Show Me the MONEY

BUSINESS

GOLD

TAX

TRADE

CURRENCY

RESOURCES

ECONOMY

VALUE

MONEY

Editors Zahavit Shalev and Fleur Star
Designed by Laura Roberts-Jensen, Hedi Gutt, Karen Hood
Publishing manager Bridget Giles
Picture Researcher Harriet Mills
Production controller Claire Pearson
Production editor Clare wMcLean
Americanization Margaret Parrish
Consultant Anthony Reuben

Dedication

To **Stephanie Jackson**, for her friendship and her enthusiasm for my work, and to my friends' young children: **Ben Farmbrough, Sam Farmbrough, Lara Howe, Sam Levinthal, Alex McKenzie, Jamie McKenzie, Jaya Saggar, Rhia Saggar, Avery Woods Weber, Jakob Woods Weber**—and the many others around the world who I hope will enjoy and benefit from this book.

REVISED EDITION

Senior editors Fleur Star, Sreshtha Bhattacharya
Senior art editors Spencer Holbrook, Ranjita Bhattacharji
US editor Allison Singer
Editor Agnibesh Das
Assistant art editor Kshitiz Dobhal
DTP designer Sachin Gupta
Senior DTP designer Harish Aggarwal
Jacket designer Surabhi Wadhwa
Jacket assistant Claire Gell
Jacket design development manager Sophia MTT
Producer, pre-production Gillian Reid
Producer Vivienne Yong
Managing editors Linda Esposito, Kingshuk Ghoshal
Managing art editors Philip Letsu, Govind Mittal
Publisher Andrew Macintyre
Publishing director Jonathan Metcalf
Associate publishing director Liz Wheeler
Design director Stuart Jackman

First American Edition, 2008
This edition published in the United States in 2016 by
DK Publishing, 345 Hudson Street, New York, New York 10014

Foreword copyright © 2008 Alvin Hall
Copyright © 2008, 2016 Dorling Kindersley Limited
DK, a Division of Penguin Random House LLC

15 16 17 18 19 10 9 8 7 6 5 4 3 2 1
001—285065—January/2016

A catalog record for this book is available from the Library of Congress.
ISBN: 978-1-4654-4000-6

DK books are available at special discounts when purchased in bulk for sales promotions, premiums, fund-raising, or educational use. For details, contact:
DK Publishing Special Markets, 345 Hudson Street, New York, New York 10014
SpecialSales@dk.com

Printed and bound in China

A WORLD OF IDEAS:
SEE ALL THERE IS TO KNOW

"
Where does money come from and how does it work?
Is money simply a tool that allows you to be paid and
to buy things you want? How does money grow?

I began to wonder about these questions when I was young,
the first time I was given a bill worth more than I could ever
have imagined. I wanted to save it and spend it at the same time.
I can still remember sitting there fascinated, staring again and
again at the money and the big number on it.

Similar questions came to me when I took my first job in the world of
finance. This time they were prompted not by big bills, but by the big
amounts of money people I had gone to college with had accumulated.
Some had become, not just millionaires, but billionaires. "How many
zeros is that?" was probably my first thought. But my second thought
was what did my old friends know about money that
I didn't? What had they learned that I had overlooked?

These last two questions launched a journey to learn more about
money, how it works and if, indeed, "money makes the world go
round." My journey has proved to be more fun, more informative,
and more enriching than I could have imagined. And that's what I'm
sharing with you in this book. Let it guide you, entertain you, and
inspire you while showing you how money works and how you can
help it work for you in the ways you want.

To your future, rich in all ways!
"

Alvin Hall

ALVIN HALL

CONTENTS

THE STORY OF MONEY

" If you were on a desert island, no amount of money would help you survive— you couldn't eat it, drink it, use it to build a shelter, or to keep away wild animals.

So why is money valuable? The answer is simply that everyone has agreed it is. Agreeing that money is valuable means we can use it to help us buy and sell things. Although it's so useful, astonishingly, no one person invented money. It just sort of happened… **"**

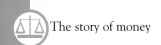

What is MONEY?

We know that money is **dollars** and **cents** (or pounds and pence, or euros and cents...)—but what is it *used for?*

Money is a *medium of exchange.* (In other words, money is used to buy stuff.)

Money is a *store of value.* (In other words, it can be saved up and used at a later date.)

Money is a *unit of account.* (In other words, a way of showing what things are worth.)

Before money people all traded what they owned. If you had too much milk, for instance, but not enough wheat, you would swap some of your milk for some wheat. The trouble is you have to find someone who wants exactly what you have and has exactly what you want. Buying and selling using money makes it easier to strike a deal, or trade. It's also much simpler if you introduce something that everyone will accept. The something else is called a medium of exchange. Now trade looks more like this: I sell my cow to someone for 10 units of something. Then I can give you ten units of something for your pig. We can both use our units to buy whatever we want from whomever we want whenever we want.

Saving up

Once you've **sold** your cow, you can *save* your five units and use them to buy something at a *later date*. If the units **KEEP** their value, you will be able to buy another cow with them in a year's time. You might earn *interest* on the money you have saved—but there is also a danger that the price of cows will go up, say, to six units. (This is called *inflation* and you can learn more about it on page 43.) If this happens, your money will have **LOST** some of its value.

What's it worth?

There are two cars in a showroom. One has a price tag of $4,000 and the other costs $12,000. By *comparing the prices*, you can quickly see that the $12,000 car is worth **more** (and therefore should be a bigger or better car). The owner of the showroom can also use the unit of account for her business records. Now instead of saying that she has **15 cars**, she can say she has **$180,000-worth** of cars.

Deal or no deal?

... or how people invented money

Directly exchanging your goods for someone else's is called *bartering*. But bartering suffers from a serious problem— you need to find someone who's *got* what you *want* and who *wants* what you've *got*. Oh, and you can't give change either. The solution is brilliant really—**money**. Here's why...

Bob does some thinking...	The next day	EUREKA!
Adding more links to the chain helps.	You can swap your stuff for something else	... and use that instead.

	CENTURIES LATER	At the bank
	Carting coins around was awkward and risky.	So people left their coins at a bank

Way, way back...

DEAL

Some time later

NO DEAL

Before there was money people used to barter...

... but they soon ran into difficulties.

A tale as old as time...

DEAL

MONEY IS INVENTED

TIME PASSES

People realized they needed to swap something that everyone wanted.

EUREKA!

DEAL

PAPER MONEY IS INVENTED

... and shopped with banknotes!

To be continued...

Banknotes don't have any value in themselves. Originally they represented something of real value (usually gold or another precious metal) sitting in the bank's vaults. These days there isn't enough gold in the world for banks to keep reserves equal to all the money in circulation. That means you can't swap your notes for gold. In fact, the money we use these days only has value because we all believe that it does!

11

From *cows* to *coins*

We know money as **notes** and **coins**, but the earliest currency wouldn't fit in your *pocket!*

Cows

It all began with people exchanging things like cows for other things they wanted under a barter system.

Silver ingots

Pieces of silver, weighed to exact amounts, were used as money in many areas of the world. China was among the earliest to do this, in 5000 BCE.

Silver ingots

Cowrie shells

The Chinese character for money is based on the cowrie shell, which was used as currency from around 1200 BCE.

Cowrie shells

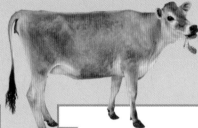

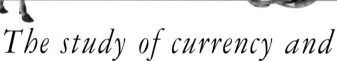

The study of currency and

9000 BCE   3000 BCE

Just make sure to get a receipt when you buy anything!

OK. Thanks, God.

Juno Moneta

BANKING BEGINS HERE

As far back as 3000 BCE, people in Babylonia used to store their valuables in temples for safekeeping. In 1800 BCE, King Hammurabi established a code of laws to ensure people traded fairly. Babylon was a trade hub, so many laws dealt with the proper way to do business, what to do when deals go wrong, and the importance of keeping records.

In Rome I am a hero!

This stone monument shows King Hammurabi receiving the Code from the Sun God.

Next time you're searching and fumbling for the right change, just remember that money is pretty convenient compared to some of the alternatives...

King of Lydia

Any chance of a **gold coin** for all this hard work?

The coin king

King Croesus of Lydia was famed for his wealth. He is said to have invented the world's first system of money with two levels of coins: gold and silver.

Model tools

Early on, useful things, like tools, functioned as money. Over time model spades or knives replaced the real thing. Model tools were used in China between 1000 and 500 BCE.

Knife-shaped coin

Electrum coins

The first recognizable coins were made around 640 BCE in Lydia (present-day Turkey). They were made of electrum, a naturally occurring mix of silver and gold.

Electrum coins

Paper money

The first paper money was used 1400 years later in China, in 800 CE. So many notes were made that they became worthless and had been abandoned by 1455.

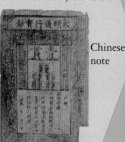

Chinese note

its history is called "numismatics."

390 BCE 323 BCE 800 CE

This isn't money. This is lunch.

GAULS VS. GEESE

The ancient Romans kept their reserves of money in the Capitol building. In 390 BCE, an attack on the Capitol building by gold-seeking Gauls was thwarted—by geese! The birds' honking alerted the Romans, who believed that the geese were sent by Juno Moneta, the goddess of warning. It is from her name that we get the word "money."

HONK!
HONK!
HONK!

STATE GRANARIES

In ancient Egypt, grain was used as currency and local granaries functioned as banks. Records of all transactions were kept at the central granary in Alexandria. Using these accounts, people were able to transfer grain from one person to another. Today, a similar process is done with money and is called a "credit transfer."

Yum!

Silk and spice & all things nice — 100 miles

Money *makes* the world go AROUND...

The Middle Ages saw an exploration **explosion**. *Adventurers* and *merchants* traveled the world opening up new *trade routes*, **discovering** new products, and bringing back **ideas** and **loot**.

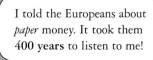
Land **AHOY**!

Polo
(1254–1324)

1275

I told the Europeans about *paper* money. It took them **400 years** to listen to me!

POLO MAKES A MINT

When Marco Polo traveled from Europe to China along the Silk Route, he was amazed to see the Chinese using paper money. At that time, Europe only used gold and silver. He might have been even more surprised by some of China's earlier ideas for currency, including cowrie shells, tools, and large pieces of white deerskin.

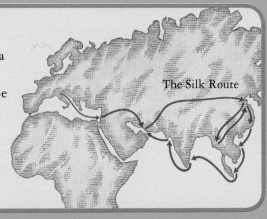
The Silk Route

PEPPER was a **valuable** *commodity* for traders

BEWARE
BANDITS!

COMMERCIAL TRADE

Traders could sell more if they took their goods to places where people didn't produce the same goods. But traveling was risky and time-consuming, so it had to be worth making the journey. The solution was to take large amounts—and so commercial trading was born. By the 4th century BCE, there was a regular Incense Route across Asia and Europe.

COLUMBUS THE CONTRARY

The age of exploration was in full swing, driven by the desire to trade. Importing valuable silk and spices from China and India involved a long and dangerous journey, what with bandits, pirates, storms at sea, and other shipping threats. It was also expensive: there was no such thing as free trade, and every time a ship from one country passed through a port belonging to another country, a tax was charged for the cargo. Columbus decided to try a new route: straight across the "Ocean Sea"—the Atlantic—a scary thought in an age of myths and monsters, when some people believed you'd die if you crossed the equator.

Columbus
(1451–1506)

1492   1498   1519

Cortés
(1485–1547)

OLD SPICE RETURNS

Between the precious Indian spices and the European traders stood the Moors of North Africa, who had the monopoly on trading spices. The Portuguese wanted their own control, so explorer Vasco da Gama was sent to open up the sea route to India. Portugal established its own colonies around the African coast and charged taxes on trade that passed through.

Vasco da Gama (1460–1524)

EL CONQUISTADOR

Although spices were as valuable as gold, gold was still important as currency. Spanish adventurer Hernando Cortés sailed halfway around the world in pursuit of gold, conquering the Aztecs of South America. He plundered the land for anything he could ship back to Spain.

at times worth *more than* its weight in gold.

Tricks of the trade

With even more **opportunities** for international trade, business was **booming**. *Currencies* **began to be standardized**, making trade **simpler** and **fairer**.

STOCK EXCHANGES

Companies raise money by selling shares (see page 26). In return, investors receive a share in future profits. The first shares issued were for the Dutch East India company, and they were traded at the first official stock exchange building in Amsterdam in 1602. Before that, traders used to meet in and outside coffee houses to conduct business.

TULIP MANIA

Exotic goods can sell for high prices. Middle-class Dutch people got involved in trading tulips—a new import from Turkey—on the stock market, sometimes even selling their homes to do so. But prices dropped by as much as 90 percent in 1637, and fortunes were lost.

1602   **1637**   Adam Smith (1723–1790)   **1776**

Shake my *invisible* hand!

A HELPING HAND

Adam Smith is considered the grandfather of economics. In his 1776 work *An Inquiry into the Nature and Causes of the Wealth of Nations*, he argued that a free market results in the greatest good for society overall. When people are free to act in their own interests, they are guided by an "invisible hand" to do things that are good for society, too, such as making products that people need.

Capitalism vs **Communism**

Marx viewed capitalism as the way upper-class people profit from working-class people. Workers are paid wages, says Marx, but they produce more than they are paid for. The extra goes to their bosses, who get rich. With communism, everything is shared; no one owns property, and so no one can be exploited.

> *Workers of the world unite. You have nothing to lose but your chains!*

The dollar

The US Coinage Act in 1792 made dollars and cents the only formal units of currency in the United States of America. Before the Act, different states had their own currencies. For example, in Virginia they used tobacco leaves (and later on, the notes issued for tobacco deposited in warehouses). In 1794, the US Mint opened in Philadelphia, the capital at that time.

An early dollar

Karl Marx
(1818–1883)

1792   1816

A sovereign was a £1-coin made of gold.

Good as gold

In 1816, the British Government introduced the gold standard, where the value of the currency was tied to a specific weight of gold. If you had a banknote worth £1, you could exchange it at a bank for £1-worth of gold. Many countries adopted the gold standard, and it became the international standard against which all currencies could be measured. Britain abandoned the gold standard in 1931, but the US held onto it until 1973.

Karl Marx

Not everyone thought capitalism was a good idea. After spending 30 years studying the capitalist way of working in England (the most advanced industrial society of his day) Marx published his thoughts in *The Communist Manifesto* and *Das Kapital*, and communism was born.

Gold bullion

Modern money

The 20th century was a time of change. *Governments* became more closely involved in **economic policies** across the world, and even money changed... from **gold** to *plastic!*

Problem number one: not everyone works. Problem number two: some people have more money than others. I say, let the government sort it out. (Isn't that what they're there for?)

KEYNES'S GENERAL THEORY

In the 1770s, Adam Smith (the one with the invisible hand) promoted "laissez faire" ("leave it alone") politics. He wanted governments to leave trade alone and not interfere with the economy. But 160 years later, another economist, Keynes saw this wasn't working. The solution, according to his *General Theory* was the opposite—governments should intervene! When things get tough, said Keynes, the government should borrow money to spend on public works and lowering taxes. Then, when the economy recovers, it can pay back the loans.

John Maynard Keynes
(1883–1946)

1931   1936   1944

UN flag

LET IT BE

In the 1930s, many countries gave up the gold standard. (The US waited until 1973.) Now that currency wasn't tied to the price of gold, banknotes were no longer "representative money"—they didn't represent amounts of gold any more. Instead, banknotes became "fiat money," which is money that is valuable simply because the government says it is, and everyone else agrees. The word "fiat" means "let it be"—in other words, we allow money to have value even though a banknote isn't really worth anything itself.

THE BRETTON WOODS AGREEMENT

At a conference held in Bretton Woods, New Hampshire, the United Nations agreed to set up three organizations to help international trade after World War Two (which ended in 1945). These are: the International Monetary Fund, the International Bank for Reconstruction and Development, and the General Agreement on Tariffs and Trade.

Frank McNamara (1917–1957)

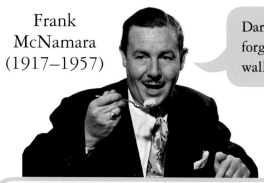

Darling, I've forgotten my wallet again...

PUT IT ON THE CARD

In 1949, in New York City, Frank McNamara went to pay his restaurant bill at the end of a meal... but he had forgotten his wallet! To save other people from suffering the same embarrassment, a year later he set up the Diners Club. When club members ate in a restaurant, instead of paying for their meal, they would show their Diners Club membership card. The restaurant would bill the Club instead, and the Club would bill the customer later. And so the credit card was born. (As for Frank's bill— his wife paid!)

A modern Diners-Club card

NEW YEAR, NEW EURO

On January 1, 1999, 11 countries in the European Union adopted the euro as their currency. But people in Austria, Belgium, Finland, France, Germany, Ireland, Italy, Luxembourg, the Netherlands, Portugal, and Spain couldn't spend any euros because there were no coins and notes until 2002! (They continued to use their country's currency instead.) The euro was one of the outcomes of the European Monetary System, which was created in 1979 to protect European countries' economies from high inflation, and to help international trade.

1950   1967   1999

ATMs

Many people claim to have invented the first Automated Teller Machine (ATM), but the credit goes to John Shepherd-Barron for creating the first machines that actually dispensed money. He based his design on a chocolate machine (an idea he had while in the bathtub). The first ATM appeared in London, but it didn't use plastic cards like today's ATMs. Instead, you had to insert a voucher made from radioactive paper to show how much money should be taken from your bank account.

If I can get chocolate from a machine, why can't I get money from one?

John Shepherd-Barron (1925–2010)

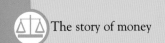

ALL the money

FUNNY MONEY

Tools and cowries were common currency in the past, but they weren't the only unusual forms of money. In central Africa, you could have purchased a wife for 50 bells! Since around 1960, nearly every form of what's called "primitive money" has been replaced with modern money, which makes it much easier to trade internationally.

Emergency money

In the past, shortages of coins and banknotes led to some interesting stand-ins. In the 17th century, the governor of Canada paid his troops with playing cards instead of coins. The cards were cut up and written on, and could be exchanged for goods in stores.

Manillas

In the 1500s the Portuguese were busy sending huge quantities of copper and brass to West Africa to be turned into currency. They didn't become coins, but manillas, or bracelets. It was much easier to wear metal than to carry it. Manillas were decommissioned (no longer legal tender) in 1949, when they were worth around 7 cents each.

Wampum

Strings of clam-shell beads, called wampum, were used by North American Indians. The most common beads were white; purple beads were far more rare, and therefore more valuable. In 1760, a factory began to mass produce the beads. Soon there were so many, the value of the beads fell and they stopped being used as currency.

Fei stones

This money, from the Island of Yap in the Pacific Ocean, may be the only form of primitive money still in use today. In fact, it is mostly used for ceremonial purposes. Fei stones can be 12 ft (3.5 m) tall, and to move one, a long pole is put through the hole in the middle so it can be rolled along. It's not pocket change!

HOW MUCH MONEY IS THERE IN THE WORLD?

It's impossible to answer this question! The amount of physical money changes all the time as notes and coins are made and lost or wear out. Also, exchange rates—how much the money is worth compared to other currencies—change every day. Today, $1 might be worth £0.50, but tomorrow it might be £0.40 or £0.70. To make it easier to compare value, there needs to be a universal currency, and for centuries it was gold.

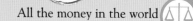

in the WORLD

BUREAU DE CHANGE

If you go on vacation abroad, you may need to exchange your currency for one of around 180 others used in the world.

Country	Currency	Made up of...	Symbol
China	yuán	10 jiao	元
Cuba	peso	100 centavos	₱
India	rupee	100 paisa	₹
Israel	shekel	100 agorot	₪
Japan	yen	100 sen	¥
Kenya	shilling	100 cents	Sh
Saudi Arabia	riyal	100 halala	﷼
Thailand	baht	100 satang	฿
United Kingdom	pound	100 pence	£
Vietnam	dong	10 hao	đ
see list below...	euro	100 cents	€

As of January 2015, 19 European countries use the euro: Austria, Belgium, Cyprus, Estonia, Finland, France, Germany, Greece, Ireland, Italy, Latvia, Lithuania, Luxembourg, Malta, the Netherlands, Portugal, Slovakia, Slovenia, and Spain. The list will continue to grow as more countries in Europe officially adopt the euro as their currency.

Dollars and cents

From the Americas to Africa and Australasia, many countries all over the world use dollars and cents as their currency—but these dollars are not all the same. At the time of writing this book, one United States dollar is worth nearly 8 Hong Kong dollars.

SO HOW MUCH GOLD IS THERE IN THE WORLD?

Sorry, but we can't really answer this one accurately either! But we can try to work it out. In one year, 50 million troy ounces (that's the measurement of gold) is produced, which is enough to make a cube 14 ft (4.3 m) along each side, weighing 3 million lbs (1½ million kilograms). That's just about large enough to fill the living room of an average house. Today, that cube would be worth about $13 billion, but its value changes all the time. What we don't know is how much gold has been produced throughout history. A good guess would be a cube between 62 ft and 82 ft (20 m and 25 m) along each side—which means the total amount of gold ever discovered would fit into a tennis court.

Coin factories

The first coins were manufactured back in the 7th century BCE. A lump of metal was "minted" (stamped) with a seal to prove its value. In those days each coin was made by hand, often out of gold or silver. Today, most coins are made of metals chosen for their strength. Heavy-duty machinery is used to cut out the metal disks and punch out the designs using a huge amount of pressure.

Licensed to print

Printing paper money also requires a lot of special equipment. Europe's first official banknotes were issued in Sweden in 1660. Banknote printing houses produce their own paper, which must be strong and incorporate a number of security features. They use many other complex techniques including holograms, tiny writing, metallic strips, and up to five different printing techniques to produce banknotes. New technologies are constantly being developed to keep ahead of counterfeiters (people who make fake money).

Preparing to press

The main design of most banknotes is printed from an engraved steel plate. The detailed engraving must be done in reverse so that it prints the right way around on the paper.

Making

If it were really simple,

Complex colors

The colors on this banknote are mixed from 22 inks—including some invisible inks.

Layer upon layer

The design is built up using various different printing methods.

One and only

Each and every banknote has its own unique serial number.

Feels good!

Traditional banknotes are made of cotton fiber and linen. Some countries now use plastic instead.

Ghostly marks

A watermark is actually part of the paper. If you hold the note up to the light, a pale image appears.

Magic thread

Plastic or metal thread is woven through most banknotes. The "stitches" can be seen on both sides of the note, and appear as a solid line if you shine a light through the paper.

MONEY

everyone would be doing it!

Now you see me...

Most notes include "invisible" features that only show up under infrared or ultraviolet light.

How much?

Every note clearly states its value in a number of places.

JA123456

3-D images

Many banknotes feature a hologram, a type of photograph that shows an object in three dimensions. If you tilt the note, you should be able to see it.

Sign here please

Notes often feature the signature of the chief cashier or president of the national bank. Before notes were printed, each note would be signed by hand.

FAKES AND FORGERIES

People have tried to make their own money ever since coins were first introduced.

Clipping coins

Most coins have ridges around the edge. That's because when coins were made of gold and silver, people used to shave off bits of metal from the edges, melt them down, and then turn them into new coins. Ridges made it easy to detect if a coin had been clipped.

Superdollars

The superdollar is an almost-perfect forgery of an American dollar bill. Millions of superdollars were thought to have been created in Communist North Korea during the 1990s and were perhaps intended to destabilize the US economy.

This forged 1868 Swedish banknote was completely hand drawn.

Do not destroy

In many countries there are laws, not just against forgery (making fake money), but forbidding people from defacing (damaging) money. That's because printing money is an expensive business! More importantly, being able to trust that the money in circulation is genuine is necessary for the economy. How could we buy and sell things if we were not sure that the money we were using was real?

23

ELECTRONIC MONEY

A great deal of the money that circulates in society is invisible. It enters and leaves bank accounts without ever becoming notes and coins. When people make big purchases it is scarcely ever in "hard cash" and usually takes the form of an electronic money transfer by credit or debit card or by check.

Credit and debit cards are accepted almost everywhere. Simpler than cash, they're...

FANTASTIC

Until the 1950s, to *buy something* you needed to pay for it with cash. Then there were checks (see page 33). But credit and debit cards have truly revolutionized *shopping*. These days we use actual coins and notes less and less, and pretty soon they will seem as *old-fashioned* as shells and beads.

VALID FROM ▶ **01/15** EXPIRES END ▶ **01/17**

MISS C CARD

SORT CODE ▶ **01 23 43**

To prevent fraud, the cardholder's name appears on the card to show who should be using it. The card cannot be used after its expiration date.

Never mind the change

There are many ways people benefit from electronic banking. "Putting it on the plastic" (using a card to pay in a store) saves people from having to get, and carry around, actual notes and coins.

Safety in numbers

Every card has a hologram to make it hard for counterfeiters to make fake cards. It appears behind the long number that runs across the middle of the card. The first six digits of this number identify which company issued the card, the next set are the cardholder's account number, and the last digit is the "check," a security feature to prevent counterfeiters making up random card numbers.

PLASTIC!

Online banking

Instead of going into a bank, people can go online or phone their bank to access their accounts. You can check your balance (how much money you have), pay bills, and do nearly everything you can do in a branch, except get actual cash!

Automated Tellers

Even more convenient than online banking, ATMs make it possible for you to deposit (pay in) and withdraw (take out) real money, in addition to paying bills. There are more than 1.6 million ATMs in the world—there's even one in Antarctica!

PICK A CARD...

Debit cards take money straight out of your bank account—it's like paying for things with cash. Credit cards allow you to spend money loaned to you by the bank, although you will have to pay it back! Credit means you are spending money you may not actually have. You usually end up paying back more than you borrowed because of interest charges.

A debit card features an account number (linking the card to the cardholder, and a sort code (which links it to a particular bank.)

ACCOUNT NUMBER ▶ 87654321

Playing the market

Companies issue securities on the **stock market** to raise money to invest in the business. There are two types of securities: *shares* (also known as common stock) and *bonds*. People can buy and sell shares through a **stock exchange**.

A changing market
Prices of securities change all the time because people want to buy and sell them. If there are more sellers than buyers, prices will fall. If there are more buyers than sellers, prices will rise.

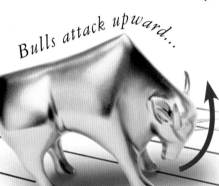

Bulls attack upward...

The bull...
If an investor feels "bullish," they want to buy, buy, buy. This is because they expect the price of a security, a commodity, or the overall stock market to rise.

... and the bear
"Bearish" investors expect the price of a security, a commodity, or the overall stock market, to decline.

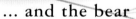

... bears attack downward

Investing is a process of **choosing** where to put your money so it will make you *the most money* at a level of **risk** you are prepared to take. Some *investments* have the potential to make *lots of money* but you could **lose everything**.

SHARES
Shares represent ownership in a company. If a company issues 100 shares and you buy 5 of them, you own 5 percent of that company. As a shareholder, you may receive a dividend (part of the company's profits), and you have the right to vote at shareholder meetings. The value of the shares can rise and fall with the fortunes of the company. If company does well, the value of your shares could rise. But if the company does badly, the value of your shares could fall.

Traditional exchanges had a central trading floor where traders executed orders given to them by their customers. There are only a few exchanges that still use trading floors today.

buy

Getting noticed
With hundreds of traders all trying to get each others' attention, the trading floor is a busy, noisy place. Traders wear colorful jackets to be noticed.

BONDS

When you buy a company's bonds you are lending money to the company. In return, the company promises to pay you a fixed rate of interest and, on a given date, the company promises to repay the exact amount it borrowed from you.

FUTURES

In addition to stock exchanges, there are other exchanges where futures are traded. With a futures contract, a trader agrees to buy a certain amount of a product, such as gold, foreign currencies, or even pork bellies, at a particular price on an agreed upon date in the future. Futures were first created so farmers could sell their crops for a prearranged price ahead of harvest.

The disappearing trading floor

The traditional world of a trading floor has almost entirely disappeared. Today, most exchanges use computerized systems that have totally replaced the trading floor and many of the people on it. A trader can now work from a desk using multiple computer screens. An automated exchange system makes it easier and quicker to execute orders to buy and sell securities. The computers monitor the different markets where the securities are being traded and automatically match a buyer and a seller in a given stock, bond, or future. It's a less colorful, but more efficient way of trading.

Yelling and using **hand signals,** they make the other traders aware that they have an order, for example, to sell specific stock, and try to find

PUT
A put gives the buyer the right to *sell* stock at a prearranged price.

CALL
The opposite of a put, a call gives the buyer the right to *buy* stock at a

MONTHS
Futures contracts have a month when they expire. These hand signals

NUMBERS
These show the number of contracts being offered.

Trading *WITHOUT*

The earliest form of trading took place without money. If *goods* and *services* are available to trade, and modern communications can make trade possible across a large area, is cash no longer necessary? Can we live in a *cashless* economy?

The old ways are best

Traditional barter continues today, mostly among cash-poor communities where money isn't readily available. If a farmer grows more crops than his family can eat, he may trade the excess for meat from a local butcher.

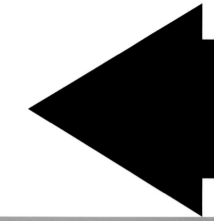

At your service

Services can also be bartered: a hairdresser may be "paid" in jars of jam rather than in cash; or a chef might cater a party for a bricklayer in return for building a wall.

Being "cash poor" isn't the same as being poor—you

A CASHLESS ECONOMY?

Instead of paying for things with cash, we can use an electronic transfer instead. However, it is highly unlikely that we will get rid of cash forever because it is so convenient, especially if you are too young to have a bank card!

Cash is being used less and less as people increasingly use credit and debit cards to buy things.

Virtual money

 -$100

When a person buys something using a debit card, the bill is deducted from that person's bank account without money changing hands. But debit cards aren't the only form of electronic transfer...

 +$100

Chances are, you've traded without money yourself. Have you ever swapped your egg sandwiches for your friend's cheese ones? Or traded stickers in the school playground? If so, you've successfully bartered.

MONEY

LETS do a deal

Local Exchange Trading Systems (LETS) is a modern form of barter. People build up credits in exchange for providing goods or services, and then use the credits to buy what they need. Credits are recorded so everyone can see them, but they cannot be cashed in for real money.

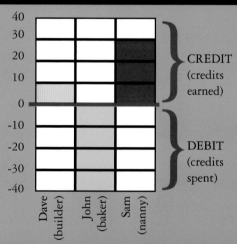

CREDIT (credits earned)

DEBIT (credits spent)

How does it work?

Let's say Dave builds a wall for John, at an agreed for price of 20 credits. John also pays Sam 20 credits for childcare. Now John owes 40 credits in total. Next, Dave asks Sam to babysit, and pays her 10 credits. Now Sam has 30 credits, and Dave is left with 10.

There is a type of LETS that operates worldwide.

don't need lots of money to have a good quality of life.

Don't stop!

Drivers can put radio frequency identification (RFID) tags in their cars. When the car passes through a tollgate, the tag automatically charges the toll to the driver's credit card.

Cash calls

A system is being tested where people use cell phones to make purchases. Money transferred from their bank account is stored in the phone as credits that can be used to buy goods.

Speedy payment

Lots of people in the US use an RFID key fob, called a Speedpass, to pay for gas. Scanning the fob is faster than using a credit card for payment.

Store it up

Loyalty cards issued by stores can be an alternative to cash. However, to collect the points, (which you can use as payment for future purchases) you have to buy stuff in the first place!

29

WHAT'S IN YOUR POCKET?

" **Money is magical.**
People **dream** about it, **worry** about it, **fight** over it, and nobody ever seems to feel that they have **enough** of it.

Money means different things to different people. It's a reward for hard work, the gift of freedom from worry, the key to a life of luxury, a way to get an education, earn respect, or even change the world. *Money is potential.* **"**

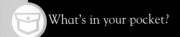

WHAT'S IN YOUR

If there's **cash** in your pocket, lucky YOU!

Before we go any further, let's figure out how it got there.

POCKET?

(Aside from dirty tissues, your house keys, and a pack of chewing gum...)

Allowance

Do you get a weekly or monthly allowance from your parents? Are there rules about what it can be spent on (clothes, books, going out), or can you buy whatever you want with it? Managing your allowance is a good way to learn about budgeting.

Thanks!

CANDY STORE

Gifts

Do your relatives sometimes give you gifts of money, as a treat, for a birthday or Christmas present, or because you got good grades? This money is yours to do whatever you want with. If these gifts come fairly regularly, they could add up to a large amount of money.

WELL DONE on passing your exams. love Grandpa x

Cool, Grandpa. My school work will make me rich!

Earnings

Do you sometimes do odd jobs like washing cars or babysitting? Do you have a paper route? According to the law, children are only allowed to do certain kinds of jobs. Still, money you get from these jobs is money that you have earned, just like the money your parents earn from their jobs.

Good job! You've really earned this.

WHAT'S IN YOUR PARENTS' POCKETS?

As well as cash, your parents have other forms of money in their wallets. Most adults have credit cards, debit cards, and store cards.

Cards are convenient, but if you use them incorrectly they can be confusing and costly.

Cards

Cards allow you to buy things without using cash. With store cards and credit cards you buy goods now, and pay for them at the end of the month. You have to pay interest if you don't pay in full. Debit cards take money directly from your account when you make a purchase.

Checks

A check is a written instruction to pay someone a specific amount of money. Checks are becoming less common now that it is so easy to make electronic payments, which don't use real cash at all.

Spend, *stash,* or SAVE?

It's your birthday!

You've been given a present of **$50**. What can you do with all that money?

IMPORTANT NOTE: Some of these options aren't available to all children. In some countries, people under the age of 16 cannot open bank accounts. In many places, children would not be allowed to make investments, or can do so only with their parents' permission.

SPEND?

If there's something big you've been wanting to buy for ages that you think you'll be able to enjoy—such as a guitar—maybe now is the time to buy it. (But before you do, learn how to be a wise shopper with the tips on the next page.) Remember, once your money is gone, that's it. So think carefully about whether your purchase will actually make you happier before you take the plunge.

> $50! What shall I buy? I'll treat myself to a guitar!

$50

STASH?

If there's nothing you want right now but you're planning on spending the money very soon—say, in the coming days or weeks— you could just keep it in your wallet, a jar, or a box under your bed. But don't hang on to it for too long! Money loses value over time because of inflation (see page 43) so your $50 may buy you less in a year's time than it will now.

> I like taking my money out and counting it.

SAVE?

If there's something big you're saving for, you should put your money in the bank. While it's there, the bank will lend some of it to people who want to buy something big or start a business. These borrowers pay their loans back gradually with interest, which is the fee the bank charges them for borrowing money. The bank gives you some of the interest it makes on your money. The government makes sure the bank doesn't lose your money so there's no risk involved.

> Your money will grow slowly but steadily.

SAVINGS BANK

> Good. No risk to me.

INVEST?

If you like risk, buy some shares. If the company does well you get a share of the profits. Also, if the share price rises you can sell your shares at a profit. If the company performs badly the share price will go down. Then you can either sell at a loss or hang on, hoping things improve.

50 Share certificate
STOCKS AND BONDS, INC.

THIS IS TO CERTIFY that

> You win some, you lose some! That's life.

$50

HOW DOES YOUR MONEY GROW?

Interest

When you put your money in the bank it doesn't just sit there. The bank uses your money and pays you a small amount, for instance, 4 percent each year, in return. The longer you leave your money the more it grows.

Tend to your money...

... and watch it grow!

Compound interest

If you invest $50 at a 10 percent annual interest rate you'll earn $5 over a year, turning your $50 into $55. If you leave that money in the bank for another year, you'll earn interest on both your original $50 and on the $5 you earned in interest last year, making $60.50. This is called compounding.

The rule of 72

How long will it take to double your money? Try the rule of 72. Take 72 and divide it by the interest rate—here 10 percent. The answer, 7.2, is the number of years it will take to double your money. With a 5 percent interest rate it will take 14.4 years (72 divided by 5).

Interest rate 10%

| 1 | 7 | 14 | 29 | 58 | 115 | 230 |

YEAR

35

Spending *TIPS* for

Here are a few *hints* and *tips* on HOW to become

DO I REALLY WANT THAT?

You're shopping for candy and you see chocolate on sale. Should you buy the chocolate, or stick with the candy? Here are some things to think about:

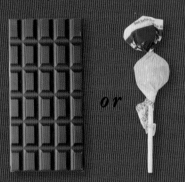

or

- $ Do I prefer chocolate instead?
- $ Is this the kind I like? It's reduced but can I actually afford the sale price?
- $ Is the chocolate cheaper than the candy? If not, should I buy the candy and save any money left over for next week's treat?
- $ Will I eat the chocolate before its "sell by" date?

> **TOP TIP**
> Make sure you actually want what you're buying.

DECIDING ON DISCOUNTS

or

Store A has a computer game for $22 with a 10% discount.

Store B has the same game for $20 and a 5% discount.

10% looks like the bigger discount. But is it the better deal? Let's do the math: 10% of $22 is $2.20, so *Store A's discounted price is $19.80*. 5% of $20 is $1, so *Store B's price is $19*.

Store B is cheaper, even though it has the smaller discount!

> **TOP TIP**
> Don't be fooled by percentages. It's the price at the end of the day that's important.

HIDDEN COSTS

Sometimes shopping costs you more than just the price written on the product.

You're in Store A looking at the game. You already know that Store B has it cheaper—but Store B is a bus ride away. It will cost you $1 for the bus, so the real cost to you of the game in Store B is $21, which is more than Store A.

 **+**  **=** MORE EXPENSIVE

> **TOP TIP**
> It's not always cheaper to chase after bargains. It may be better to buy from the store you're already in rather than make a special trip.

If you don't have the money, save up for it...

shopping *TRIPS*

a savvy, **MONEY-SAVING,** *super* shopper!

ECONOMY SIZES—IS BIGGER ALWAYS BETTER?

It's often better value to buy a large size of something than a small one—less packaging means that it works out cheaper, weight for weight.

> **TOP *TIP***
>
> Only buy the large bottle if you will finish the drink before it goes flat, or you'll end up throwing it away.

To compare prices, you need to know how much it costs to buy a certain amount of what you're buying (let's say 2 liters of soda) in all the ways you can buy it (bottles and cans).

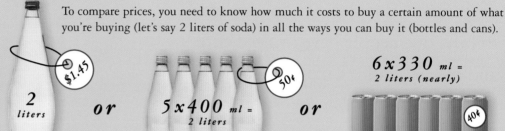

$1.45 · **2 liters** · *or* · **50¢** · **5 × 400 ml = 2 liters** · *or* · **6 × 330 ml = 2 liters (nearly)** · **40¢**

1 large bottle = $1.45   *5 small bottles at 50¢ each = $2.50*   *6 cans at 40¢ each = $2.40*

BUT IT'S ON SALE...

Although the clothes on sale are cheaper than they normally sell for, that doesn't automatically make them worth buying.

> **TOP *TIP***
>
> Don't buy stuff just because it's cheaper than normal. Look at what you're spending, not what you're saving.

💲 Do you really need new clothes? Are they similar to items you already own? Will you really wear them, or do you just think you might because they're on sale? If they just sit in your closet, they're a waste of money.

💲 Are they damaged or badly made? If there are lots of identical items in the sale, perhaps no one wants them.

💲 Think about what you're spending, not what you're saving. Let's say you find a pair of designer jeans that originally cost $300, reduced in a sale to $100. That's a saving of $200! But they still cost $100, and usually you wouldn't spend more than $40 on jeans—so that's actually $60 *extra* that you wouldn't normally spend.

over 60% off

SALE

...OR just manage   *without it.*

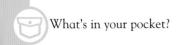
WHAT do you *want?*

There's a whole WORLD out there **full** of things to do, places to see, and stuff to buy. But people have limited time and money, and it's **impossible** to have or do *everything*. So you need to make **choices**. What you end up choosing often comes down to what makes you *happy*—but there's a whole LOT of thought that goes into that choice.

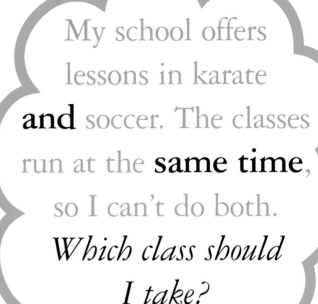

My school offers lessons in karate **and** soccer. The classes run at the **same time**, so I can't do both. *Which class should I take?*

A **cookie** costs $1 and an **ice cream** costs $1. I like *both equally*, and have $2 to spend. *What should I buy?*

The **first** is always the **best** (but the *buzz* of a new thing **wears** off *fast*).

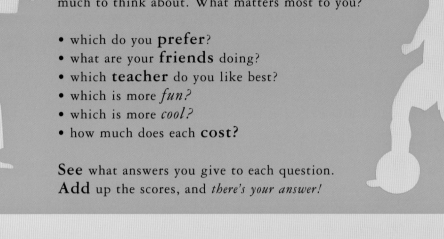

Karate *or* soccer?

This is a really complicated decision. There's so much to think about. What matters most to you?

- which do you **prefer**?
- what are your **friends** doing?
- which **teacher** do you like best?
- which is more *fun?*
- which is more *cool?*
- how much does each **cost?**

See what answers you give to each question. **Add** up the scores, and *there's your answer!*

Cookies *and* ice cream?

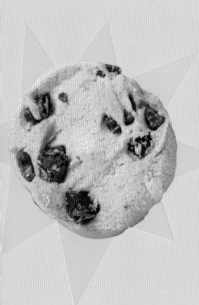

You could buy two cookies or two ice creams with your $2, but the chances are you will buy one of each. **Why?** Because the FIRST cookie (or ice cream) tastes great, but the second isn't quite so amazing. *The happiness you get from two different "firsts" is greater than the happiness you get from two of the same item.* Sometimes your decision is affected by **incentives** (things that pull you more toward one decision than the other). Suppose the ice cream costs $2. **Now** you're more likely to buy two cookies than one ice cream because you will get MORE for your money.

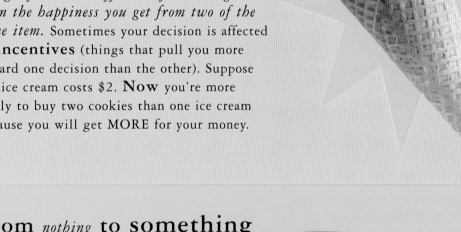

From *nothing* **to something**

Imagine you have no shoes. Walking is painful, your feet are sore and grazed. One day, you get a pair of shoes. Suddenly it feels **fantastic** to walk! Then, a week later, you get a pair of sneakers. They're nice, but not *life-changing* like the first pair. A month later, you get some flip-flops. They're ok, but they change your life *even less* than the sneakers. Why is this the case? Because *the more of something you've already got, the less of a big deal it is to get even more of it.*

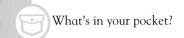

What do you NEED?

There's a difference between wants and needs. You might *want* the latest designer sneakers, but if you already own a pair of functioning sneakers you probably don't actually *need* them. When you grow up, you won't be able to spend money on treats until you've got the basics covered...

HOUSING
This is a big one. People often find themselves spending as much as a third of the money they earn putting a roof over their heads. In some countries most people rent homes; in others they buy using mortgages that can last anywhere from 10 to 40 years. Either way, it's a major expense.

TRANSPORTATION
Transportation is surprisingly costly. Think about how often your parents travel to and from work. Train tickets aren't cheap if you have to travel a long way or almost every day, neither is the cost of gas, maintenance, insurance, taxes, and tolls for a car.

THINGS I NEED:
somewhere to *live*

transportation

$20

LUXURY OR NECESSITY?
One person's "need" is another person's "want." Take owning a car. It's a big expense and not always necessary, though it can be extremely convenient.

A car might be NECESSARY if...
- You live in a place without public transportation.
- You need to transport tools or equipment in order to do your work, or your job involves a great deal of traveling.
- You have children attending a school that isn't within walking distance, or have elderly relatives who you often take to the hospital.

FOOD

Everybody needs to eat, but food costs vary wildly. You can cook from scratch (using cheaper or more expensive ingredients), buy ready-made meals, eat out in fast-food chains, or dine at fancy restaurants. Your choice determines the cost. (Cooking at home is cheapest—so learn to cook!)

CLOTHES

Strictly speaking, clothes are a necessity, but fashion is a luxury. Yet many people agree that you "need" different types of shoes and clothes for different activities. You decide!

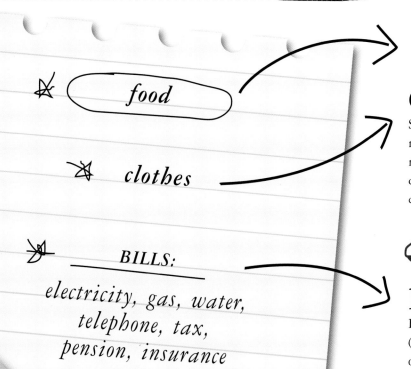

food

clothes

BILLS:

electricity, gas, water, telephone, tax, pension, insurance

$5

BILLS

Bills are paid monthly, quarterly (every three months), or annually, and often cover services such as the phone, water, and electricity. Grown-ups may grumble about bills (perhaps because you can't see services the way you can see goods) but can't avoid paying them.

But it might be a LUXURY if...

- You live in a place where you can walk or cycle to work, school, and stores.
- Public transportation is reliable and cabs are inexpensive.
- The car you have is costly to run and you have to pay for parking.

The *COST*

It's not what you've GOT that matters,

Basket of goods

Inflation is the way prices rise over time (see opposite box). To understand its effect, governments select a few hundred goods that consumers typically buy and measure the changes in their prices over time. This "basket of goods" contains various types of things:

These prices may look really cheap in today's money, but remember that people's salaries (and allowances) were very much lower, too! So these prices seemed normal in 1950.

1950

FOOD AND BEVERAGES e.g., chicken, bread, peanut butter, milk
HOUSING e.g., monthly rent, bed and bedding, electricity
CLOTHING e.g., sportswear, man's shirt, woman's dress, children's shoes
TRANSPORTATION e.g., new car, airline fare, intercity bus fare, bicycle
MEDICAL CARE e.g., dental checkup, eyeglasses, health insurance
RECREATION e.g., TV set, pet food, sports equipment, movie ticket, camera
COMMUNICATION AND EDUCATION e.g., college tuition, postage stamps, telephone services
OTHER GOODS AND SERVICES e.g., haircut, perfume, stationery, laundry services

$4

9¢

Peas

$22

3¢

22¢

$1

$3

# of LIVING

but what you can DO with it that counts.

2015

These are the kinds of prices people expect to pay for goods today. They're much higher than in 1950 because of inflation. That means that the same amount of money is worth *less* than it was in 1950.

What is inflation?

Inflation is the gradual rise in the prices of goods and services when the number of people wanting to buy those goods exceeds the supply. As one saying puts it: "Inflation is too much money chasing too few goods." As an economy grows and people's earnings increase, they can afford to spend more on the things they need and want. However, if prices start to increase at a faster rate than people's earnings, they start to buy less and the purchasing power of each dollar they earn goes down. In short, it takes more and more dollars to buy the same or fewer goods. The money you earn is worth less.

What the FUTURE *holds*

When you're a child, your *parents* look after you if you get sick But what happens to ADULTS if they get sick? And *who* takes care of them when they get old? Adults have to make *sure* they have money saved in case they need it. Here's HOW they do it...

> While I was working I put money into a well-managed pension fund each month. Now my pension payments mean I'm free to spend my time gardening and playing with my grandchildren.

A HOME OF YOUR OWN

Most people's biggest expense is somewhere to live. The choice is between renting or buying a home. Renting usually means making a monthly payment to the owner of the property. It gives people the flexibility to move and means that they do not have to be involved in the maintenance of their homes. Buying is expensive, and most people spread the cost with a type of bank loan called a mortgage. This is paid back in monthly installments over a number of years.

START SAVING NOW

People don't work their entire adult lives. Retirement (sometime between 50 and 70) means the end of earning, but not the end of spending. That's where a pension plan comes in. A pension is a special kind of investment. People pay money in while they are working. Then, after they retire, they receive a payment each month, usually for the rest of their lives. There are different types of pensions such as personal, corporate, and state.

Hope that the Sun shines, but plan for a rainy day!

IF THE WORST HAPPENS

Horrible things sometimes happen. People have accidents, and houses get broken into or catch fire. An insurance policy gives you money to help you recover. When you take out an insurance policy, you agree to pay a small amount to the insurance company each month. The company agrees to pay you if something bad happens and you need money.

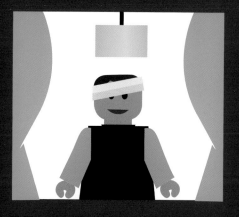

STOP THIEF! That man has broken into my house and stolen my TV set! Thank goodness I've got home insurance to pay for a new window and a new TV!

There are many forms of insurance: car insurance in case you cause an accident and have to pay to fix the other person's car (or your own); health insurance in case you get sick and have to pay costly medical bills; travel insurance in case you get sick while abroad; even pet insurance in case your pet needs expensive treatment. Insurance is a form of financial protection just in case the worst happens.

HELP TO HEAL

The money for all of our needs has to come from somewhere. Take health care: some countries, like the US, charge lower taxes and rely more heavily on private health insurance to cover medical costs. In much of Europe, however, the government collects higher taxes and uses those to pay for health care. Countries take similar approaches to childcare, education, and even social-security payments.

WINNER

Congratulations! You've won prize of $100,000 now or $10,000 a

1

> Wow! Just think of all the things I could buy with such a huge amount of money. That would make me so happy...

2

> With my lump sum, I could buy property or pay off debts so I don't have to worry about those things in the future...

3 NOW · 5 YEARS · 10 YEARS · 20 YEARS

> If inflation is high, then in 20 years time, $10,000 a year may not be worth much, so maybe I'll regret not taking the $100,000...

4 NOW

100,000 Share certificate
STOCKS AND BONDS, INC.

THIS IS TO CERTIFY that

is/are the registered holder of FIFTY Ordinary Shares of ONE DOLLAR each, fully paid, in HOODSTAR, INC

Given under the signature of the Director

Date   Signature

= THE FUTURE

> I can invest all $100,000 for the future and hope it will grow...

5 NOW · 5 YEARS · 10 YEARS

> I can put it in a bank account and get $5,000 a year interest for the rest of my life and still be able to leave the whole lump sum to my children...

takes all!

a competition and you can choose the first year for life. So—which do you choose?

$10,000 A YEAR FOR LIFE

...but I'm (hopefully) going to live for more than 10 years, so in total I'd get more than $100,000—maybe even two or three times as much.

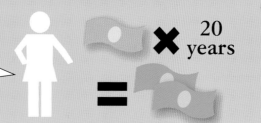

× 20 years
=

1

...although I could use the $10,000 each year to take out a mortgage to buy a house. I could also use some of the money to buy luxuries such as vacations or a better car.

2

...except that inflation might not go that high, and anyway, $10,000 is still a guaranteed income on top of my future earnings.

One day every year for the rest of my life...

3

...or I can use the annual payments to help pay my bills from now on.

2015
1. rent ✓
2. bills ✓
3. vacation
4. treats

So what's the answer?

Essentially, it's a question of how long you think you're going to live, what you think is going to happen to interest rates and inflation, and whether there is anything big such as a house that you desperately need to buy right away.

...or I can save some money each year, although the $10,000 payments will stop when I die and my children will only inherit what I've saved.

WHAT IS ECONOMICS?

“ Economics isn't
really about money!
It isn't about what we *make* or *buy,*
or even about what companies, governments,
or even entire countries *make* or *buy.*
It's about *people*, their feelings,
and behavior. And people are
the hardest things in the world
to understand. ”

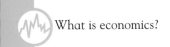

ECONOMICS IS THE STUDY OF HOW PEOPLE MAKE CHOICES.

There is lots of stuff in the world but you *can't have* everything so you *have* to make *choices.*

YOU DECIDE: should I spend my *allowance* on a *jacket* or *sneakers*?

It's your choice. Choose well!

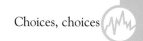

What's the best way to spend my **MONEY?**

(I want both, but I don't have enough cash.)

What do I **WANT** and
what do I **NEED?**

(I want the sneakers but I need a jacket.)

What will make me **HAPPIEST?**

(If I buy the sneakers, I will look cool,
and if I buy the jacket I will feel warm!*)*

....

Economics is *interested* in how
WE—children, adults, businesses, governments,
and entire countries—*choose.*
It also looks at the **bigger picture**
our choices create when we
add them all together.

All the STUFF

The world is **full** of *goods* and *services* we can spend our time and
and music downloads. *Services* are things you might pay p

There are four types of resources:

1 ### Natural resources
These include things we can get from nature like oil, water, air, wood, animals, and minerals. Getting them often requires a lot of effort, for instance, you've got to drill for oil and pump it out of the ground.

precious stones

rocks & minerals

water

oil

wood

There is always a cost to using resources.

2 ### Capital resources
You usually need equipment—tools, machines, and computers—to do all or part of the work. It costs money to build, buy, and maintain all this equipment.

tools

factories

transportation

THE RECIPE FO

To make anything, you have
already exist. A resource
goods or services that pec

Gather a few resources, mix them

in the world

y on. **Goods** are individual items you can buy such as books, clothes,
e to do for you such as cut your hair or coach you in soccer.

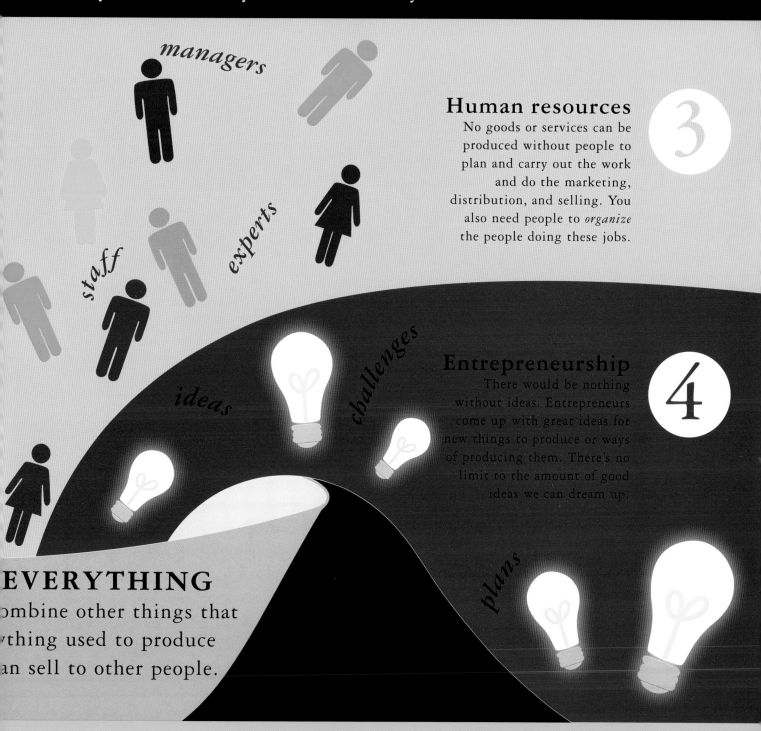

managers

staff

experts

ideas

challenges

plans

Human resources

No goods or services can be
produced without people to
plan and carry out the work
and do the marketing,
distribution, and selling. You
also need people to *organize*
the people doing these jobs.

3

Entrepreneurship

There would be nothing
without ideas. Entrepreneurs
come up with great ideas for
new things to produce or ways
of producing them. There's no
limit to the amount of good
ideas we can dream up.

4

EVERYTHING

ombine other things that
ything used to produce
an sell to other people.

together, and make something new!

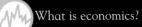

Man with a plan

...to jam in business

Mike's an *entrepreneur* with an idea. He wants to set up a business making jam to sell at the local market. There are lots of things to think about before he can achieve his goal. Many of them involve figuring out how much things will **cost**, from his *resources* to *setting the price* for the jam.

...and does some calculations

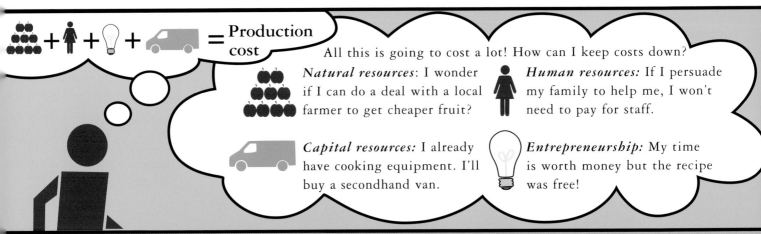

All this is going to cost a lot! How can I keep costs down?

Natural resources: I wonder if I can do a deal with a local farmer to get cheaper fruit?

Human resources: If I persuade my family to help me, I won't need to pay for staff.

Capital resources: I already have cooking equipment. I'll buy a secondhand van.

Entrepreneurship: My time is worth money but the recipe was free!

He figures out the cost of everything, including the cost of his time and effort.

Later that morning...

Pricey jam. I'd like some but not at that price.

NO DEAL

Price too high
Mike would make lots of profit with a high price, but nobody's buying the jam, so he makes no money at all.

Mike tries to sell the jam for $2 a jar.

That afternoon

That's cheap! I'll take two.

At $1 a jar, Mike sells lots of jam but his

Once upon a time...

story starts here

> I love Granny's jam. I think everyone else will love it, too. I'm going to use her recipe to make lots of jam. Then I'll sell it!

Mike is a man with an idea for a business.

Mike thinks it through...

Natural resources: Fruit and sugar to make the jam.

Human resources: A cook, and people to fill and label jars.

Capital resources: Pots, pans, jars, a delivery van.

Entrepreneurship: The idea, and Granny's recipe.

He works out what he will need.

A month later

> Now we're cooking!

Mike cooks up a batch...

The next week

> My product is ready. **I'm off to market!**

... and takes it to market.

Very early one morning...

> I reckon it costs me 90¢ to produce each jar of jam. How much should I charge?

Mike has to set the price of his jam.

BAD DEAL

> Bargain!

profit is low.

The next day

> I need to make a profit, but I also need people to buy— and they like cheap prices. I'll try selling for $1.50.

Mike sells lots of jam AND makes profit.

1 month later

> I'm in business!

Mike now sells jam in lots of markets.

To be continued...

It took Mike several attempts to figure out the best price for his jam. When the price was too high, people wouldn't buy it; but when it was too low, he made very little money even though he sold lots of jam. He didn't know it, but he was dealing with the law of supply and demand.

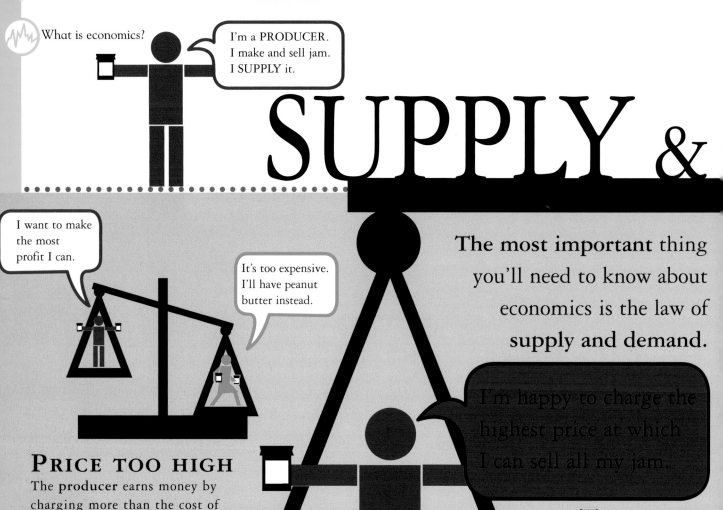

I'm a PRODUCER. I make and sell jam. I SUPPLY it.

SUPPLY &

I want to make the most profit I can.

It's too expensive. I'll have peanut butter instead.

The most important thing you'll need to know about economics is the law of supply and demand.

I'm happy to charge the highest price at which I can sell all my jam.

PRICE TOO HIGH

The **producer** earns money by charging more than the cost of production. The extra is called *profit*. Charging a high price would make plenty of profit, but the **consumer** might find it *too expensive* and **not buy** as much (or any) jam. If that happens the producer gets less (or no) profit and the consumer gets less (or no) jam.

THE PRICE

If demand goes up then either prices rise or supply goes up or a little bit of both. If producers see there is profit in jam, they start making more of it. Soon there is so much jam for sale, demand starts to fall.

Adam Smith's invisible hand

The interaction between producers and consumers— even if they don't meet— results in goods reaching their equilibrium price. This is part of what Adam Smith called the "invisible hand of the market."

Balanced supply and demand

HOW DOES DEMAND AFFECT PRICE?

Let's imagine that there are only three melons left in the market, but 12 people want to buy one. **Demand** for melons is **high**, so the trader or PRODUCER, *can charge more money* for them (as long as there are buyers). In other words, demand is high, so the price goes up. Other

High demand raises prices.

DEMAND

> I'm a CONSUMER. I want to buy jam. I DEMAND it.

The law explains why things cost what they do: *if demand is high, the price is high.* But what does that mean?

> I'm happy to pay this price for jam (but a lower price would be nicer).

IS RIGHT

This fall results in a drop in price. Eventually, the supply and demand balance out and an **equilibrium price** is reached. The producer makes a profit, the consumer can afford the jam, and everybody's happy.

> I've got lots of customers but not much profit.

> That's so cheap, I want to buy lots— but it's all gone!

PRICE TOO LOW

At a low price, jam sells well. Some **consumers** benefit from jam being *cheap*—but others who would like to buy find they can't because it's already **sold out** by the time they reach the stores. The **producer** may cover costs, but makes *little profit* despite all the jam being sold. If he raised the price, he could have made more money.

results in the equilibrium price.

...raders see that people want melons, and the next day 10 traders stock them. Now there are lots of melons in the market, many aren't being sold because there aren't enough **CONSUMERS** to buy them all—in other words, **demand is low**. In order to sell a melon, the trader has to *reduce the price* so people buy from him and not someone else. Demand has gone down, so the price has gone down.

Price changes like the weather

Prices are not fixed, they move constantly in order to reach the equilibrium price. Many factors affect price. For example, demand on umbrellas will be higher when it is raining. Suppliers could charge higher prices on rainy days.

Low demand lowers prices.

What is a FREE

I can choose how much to sell my goods for because this is a free market economy.

A free market doesn't mean you can *get stuff for free!* It means you have the freedom to trade.

WHAT IS A FREE-MARKET ECONOMY?

People who live in a free-market economy are free to make choices, and to benefit from the choices they make.

FREEDOM
People are free to choose where to live, what work to do, and who to work for.

PROFIT
Producers are allowed to sell stuff for more than it costs to make, and to keep the profit.

PRIVATE PROPERTY
The law allows people to own things, and punishes theft. This makes it worthwhile to try and make money so you can get more things.

TRADE
People can choose what to spend their money on—goods and services, savings, or investment in a business.

COMPETITION
Different businesses are free to offer similar products. This can help keep costs down for the consumer.

IS IT REALLY FREE?

Although many countries operate a free-market economy, most also have laws to stop people from doing exactly what they want. Laws prevent people from buying or selling certain goods (such as babies and illegal drugs). There are also laws that force people to give some of their profits to the government as tax.

I'm not for sale—I'm priceless.

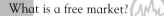

MARKET?

I think I should command some more money.

What's the opposite?

In a *command economy*, the government owns all resources, and it decides what should be made, how much should be made, and who should make it. It's no use having a good idea because even if you're allowed to carry it out, you won't get to keep any of the profits.

TOMATOES $0.80/LB

GREEN BEANS $0.95/LB

DAFFODILS $2/BUNCH

CHIVES $1/BUNCH

GREEN TOMATOES $0.60/LB

CUCUMBERS $0.30/EACH

Sunk costs

You run a flower stall. It's Friday afternoon and your flowers won't last until Monday. Someone offers you $6 for a $10 bouquet (which cost you $5). Should you sell? Yes, you've already spent $5 so $6 still means a $1 profit. What if they offer $5? Again, yes, at least you're covering your costs. $4? Well, yes again, you'll lose $1 instead of $5. The money you've already spent is a sunk cost you may never recover.

REDUCED

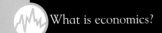

The *global* economy

Just as *producers* and *consumers trade* in a village market, countries also trade with each other. This is called the GLOBAL ECONOMY.

WHAT IS "THE ECONOMY"?

It's the way a country uses its resources, whether that's money or people or buildings. Much of the time, people use the term "the economy" to mean how much money a country has, or what a country is worth.

On a bigger scale

Economists talk about three types of market: local (your home area, perhaps a town or region), national (your country), and global (the world).

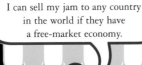

I can sell my jam to any country in the world if they have a free-market economy.

Getting the goods

Wherever goods are traded, they need to get from the producer to the consumer. This covers everything from having your groceries delivered by van, to flying and shipping goods across the globe.

What's for sale?

Of course, it's not just fruit and vegetables that are sold around the world. All kinds of commodities can be bought and sold, even human resources. In most cases, this involves transporting things from one location to another. With human resources and intangible (not physically real) commodities such as information and ideas, the actual movement of goods isn't always necessary. Technology such as phone or email can sometimes be used instead.

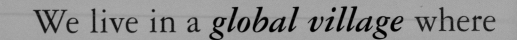

We live in a *global village* where

Big borrowing

Just like people, countries sometimes borrow money so they can buy things. The total amount a country owes is its "national debt." As with personal debt, it will need to be paid back—with interest.

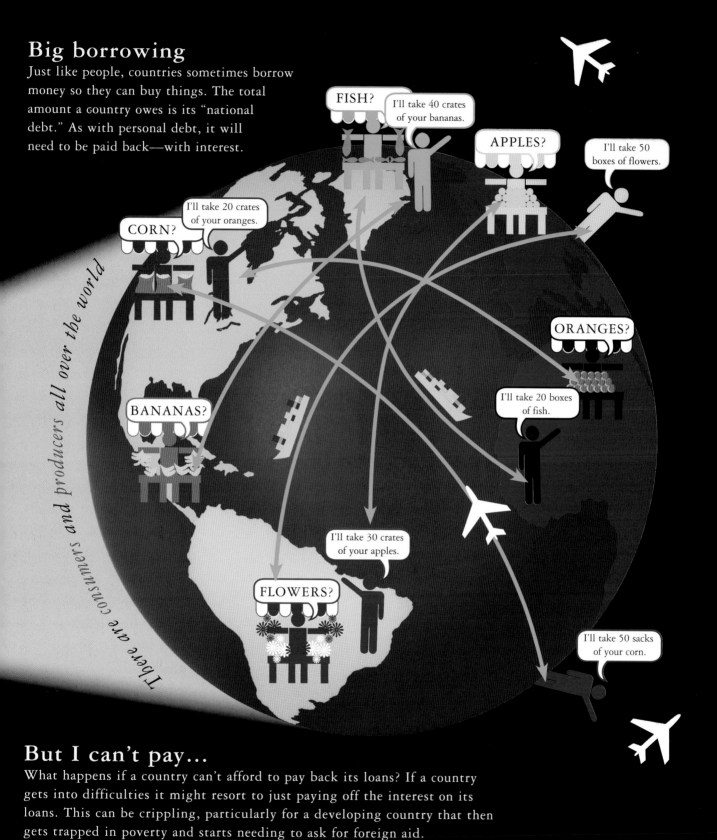

But I can't pay...

What happens if a country can't afford to pay back its loans? If a country gets into difficulties it might resort to just paying off the interest on its loans. This can be crippling, particularly for a developing country that then gets trapped in poverty and starts needing to ask for foreign aid.

trade can take place across huge distances.

Ups and *downs*

The *four seasons* of the *economy* are like the *four seasons* of the *year*. They always occur in the **SAME ORDER** but, unlike nature's seasons, the length of ***economic seasons*** are not the same, and cannot even be predicted—*although economists often try.*

INFLATION

What is inflation?

Inflation occurs when prices rise. Imagine your allowance is $10 a week, but the cost of buying a pizza goes up from $3.25 to $5. Now you can only buy 2 pizzas, when previously you could buy 3. **That's inflation!**

It's crunch time for pizzas. Chew on that!

The economic

Expansion

New businesses are opening and more jobs are being created. People feel confident in the future. Goods are being sold at home and abroad.

①

SPRING

WINTER

④

Recovery

The government lowers taxes and interest rates. People and businesses feel they have more money to spend, and gradually, as they start buying more, more jobs are created.

Prosperity

People reap the benefits of their work. Salaries increase, people have more money and are eager to spend it. But the high demand for goods leads to rising inflation.

cycle

2

SUMMER

FALL

3

Recession

Inflation causes people to buy less so company profits go down. Businesses lay off people, so unemployment rises. People earn and spend less and some can't pay their mortgages.

LOOKING FORWARD

Economic seasons are unpredictable because they are not created by the movement of money, but by the feelings people have when they think about the future. What are these feelings? Let's imagine you're about to open a present...

Optimistic

During a time of **expansion**, people feel confident about their economic future.

I think it's just what I wanted!

Concerned

After some time enjoying a period of **prosperity**, people become nervous, fearing it might end soon.

I'm not convinced I'll like this.

Pessimistic

In a time of **recession**, people feel very stressed and insecure.

This definitely isn't what I hoped for.

Cautiously hopeful

During an economic **recovery**, people begin to feel as if the worst times are coming to an end.

I'm hoping for something good.

and feelings, it's a science *and* an art.

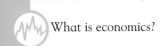

TAX

Not all *goods* and *services* are provided by companies. Some are provided by *governments*. One of the biggest decisions a government has to make is whether to provide a service (such as healthcare or education) to its citizens and fund it through a TAX, or cut taxes and let people buy it themselves from a private company.

How do governments get money?
Governments can get money in three ways. They can print it (but this leads to inflation), they can borrow it (but they'll need to pay it back), and they can collect taxes from their citizens. Taxation is the most sensible way to pay for services that everybody needs.

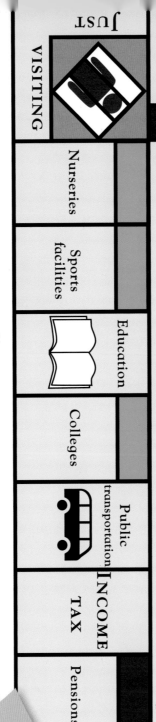

JUST VISITING

Nurseries

Sports facilities

Education

Colleges

Public transportation

INCOME TAX

Pensions

$5

But I don't pay tax!
Adults pay taxes on their earnings, but we all pay tax on the things we buy. When you buy most things, some of the price you pay goes to the government.

I'm a child. I don't pay tax!

"In this world nothing can be said to be certain, except *death* and *TAXES*"

Benjamin Franklin 1706–1790

USES FOR YOUR TAXES
Taxes help pay for the army, colleges and universities, dentists, doctors, firefighters, foreign aid, garbage collection, hospitals, the legal system, museums, the navy, nurseries, parks, pensions, police, prisons, railroads, roads, schools, social security, sports facilities, and traffic wardens.

Roads

Railroads

ROAD TAX

Airports

Emergency services

SUPER TAX

Traffic wardens

Energy

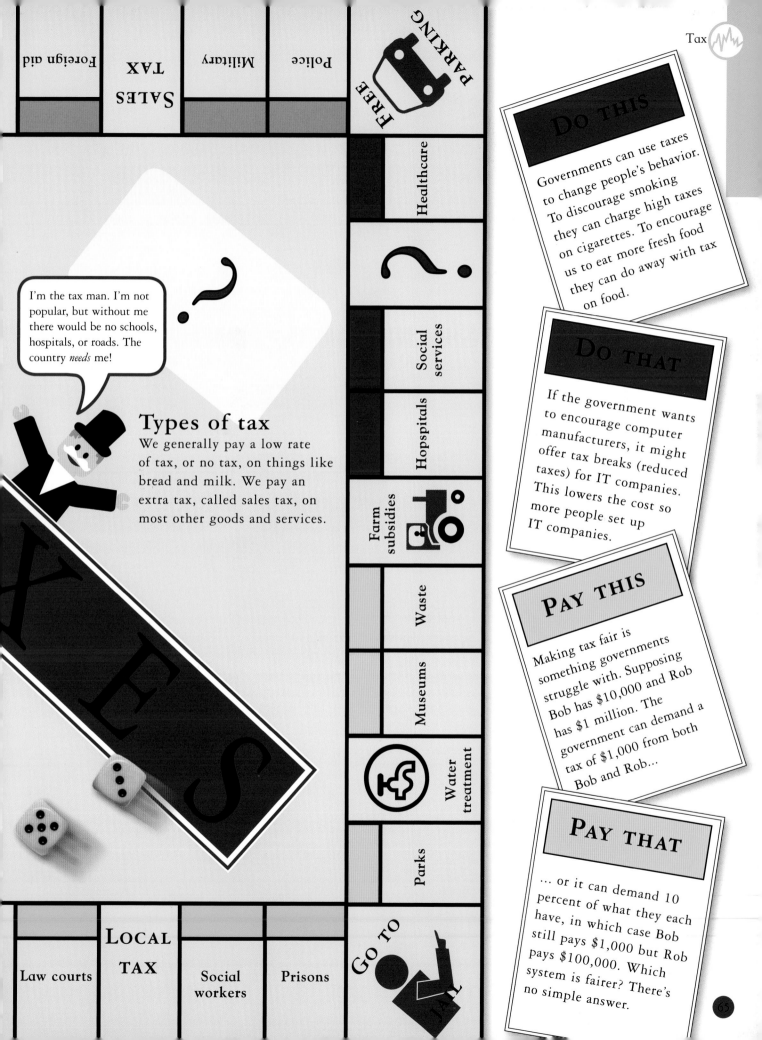

Foreign aid

SALES TAX

Military

Police

FREE PARKING

Healthcare

?

Social services

Hospitals

Farm subsidies

Waste

Museums

Water treatment

Parks

I'm the tax man. I'm not popular, but without me there would be no schools, hospitals, or roads. The country *needs* me!

Types of tax

We generally pay a low rate of tax, or no tax, on things like bread and milk. We pay an extra tax, called sales tax, on most other goods and services.

TAXES

LOCAL TAX

Law courts

Social workers

Prisons

GO TO JAIL

DO THIS

Governments can use taxes to change people's behavior. To discourage smoking they can charge high taxes on cigarettes. To encourage us to eat more fresh food they can do away with tax on food.

DO THAT

If the government wants to encourage computer manufacturers, it might offer tax breaks (reduced taxes) for IT companies. This lowers the cost so more people set up IT companies.

PAY THIS

Making tax fair is something governments struggle with. Supposing Bob has $10,000 and Rob has $1 million. The government can demand a tax of $1,000 from both Bob and Rob...

PAY THAT

... or it can demand 10 percent of what they each have, in which case Bob still pays $1,000 but Rob pays $100,000. Which system is fairer? There's no simple answer.

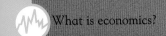

The best things

Money helps people meet their basic needs for food, clothing, shelter, and
life less hard (like dishwashers) and more fun (like vacations). Beyond that,
time, not more money. After all, you can't put a price on a hug from a

Can happiness be measured...

Measuring HAPPINESS
The government's job is to keep people safe and happy. Are
things improving? To find out start with these...
- **GDP** is the amount of goods a country produces. GDP per
person is sometimes used as a measure of well-being.
- **STANDARD OF LIVING** tells you the amount of goods
and services people in a country are using.
- **GENUINE PROGRESS INDICATOR** is based on GDP
but also considers welfare (e.g., health and crime rate).
- **HUMAN DEVELOPEMENT INDEX** looks at GDP, life
expectancy, literacy, education, and standard of living.

Kingdom of happiness
In 1972, the King of Bhutan—a
tiny Himalayan country between
China and India—came up with
Gross National Happiness
(GNH). Rather than pursue
economic growth, he said
Bhutan's policies should aim
to be economically fair,
culturally suitable, safe for
the environment, and lead
to better government.

A *treat* once in a while will make you

HOW TO BE HAPPIER
You don't need to do anything complicated to
feel happier. Try these simple rules:

Eat healthier food. You'll have more energy and feel happier.

Buy less stuff. Buying isn't satisfying; it leads to more buying!

 Watch less TV. Choose what you're going to watch.

 Spend more time with people you like.

 Think happy thoughts and make yourself smile.

in life are free

health. More money can help people get more of the pleasures that make

money doesn't tend to make people any happier. Sometimes we need more

friend or a glorious sunset.

38 39 40 41 42 43 44 45 46 47 48 49 50 51 52 53 54 55 56 57 58 59 60

...and if so, how?

6 | 8 | 7 | 9 | 5 | 4 | 3 | 2 | 1 INCH

> Happiness matters more than money so let's measure GNH, not GDP.

Happiness is relative!

If your grandma gave you $100 you'd be happy. But if you then found out she had given your sister $200 you would be annoyed. Why? You're still $100 richer! Yes, but happiness is relative. People always compare what *they* have to what *other* people have. So if you want to feel rich, either don't ask, or choose poor friends!

> I was happy for a moment, but now I just want what she's got.

> I'm happy now (but I wonder what grandma's going to give our brother...)

happier than a *treat* **every day.**

 Treat yourself, but not too often or it won't feel like a treat.

 Challenge yourself. You don't have to win.

 Do more sports. You'll sleep better, too.

Help out. Do something kind for someone else.

 Spend more time outdoors and in nature.

 Laugh! The effects last for a long time.

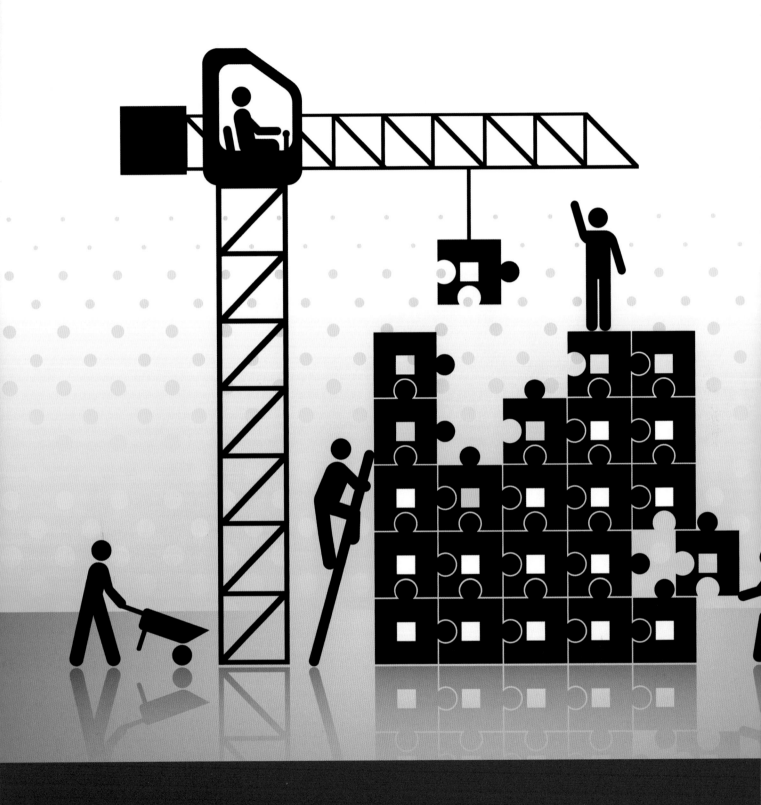

 Getting down to BUSINESS

"" **Money** makes the world go round. But ***work*** gets people **up** in the **morning** (and sometimes keeps them awake at night).

Why is work necessary?
What kinds of work are there?
How is the world of work changing?
What is the best way to get rich?
These are *good questions.*
Now read on for some answers... ""

Why WORK?

Do you like imagining *what kind of work* you will do when you grow up? What do you think you will **like** or **dislike** about work? Work is a NECESSITY for most people, but even so, the *reasons* people give for working are many and varied. So why do people work?

For the MONEY.

I like to put my skills **to good use** and be part of a **team.**

Because I *enjoy work* and like my colleagues.

I believe my work is *important.*

MINIMUM WAGE

Many countries, including the US, Canada, Australia, and much of Europe, have a minimum wage. This means that the law, not the free market, determines what the lowest paid workers should receive.

WORKING CONDITIONS

The law makes companies maintain safe working conditions for their workers. In some areas, companies compete for the best employees by offering workers benefit packages that include healthcare, pension plans, and vacation and sick pay.

DISCRIMINATION

Many countries require workers and bosses to draw up a contract describing the work to be done. Companies cannot dismiss workers without good cause. They may not discriminate between workers on the basis of gender, ethnicity, religion, or age.

WORKING HOURS

Over the last century, in some countries, laws and pressure from unions (workers' organizations) have reduced the average working week to around eight hours a day spread over five days. Before that, 14-hour days were common.

An **excellent question,** particularly as you will spend **75,000 hours** working, *over the course of your* life.

> I like to keep *busy.*

> *What are you doing here? I mean, er, no comment.*

> Well, I'm just **playing** actually...

> Because I am programmed to work.

WHEN TO STOP	BLACK MARKET	CAN CHILDREN WORK?	HAVE MACHINES STOLEN OUR JOBS?
As life expectancies are increasing, many people are choosing to work into older age. Compulsory retirement is becoming less common and people are phasing their work out more gradually.	Illegal drugs, weapons, and stolen goods get bought and sold on the "black market." Here too, children and illegal immigrants work in bad conditions for less than the minimum wage and with no job security.	In developed countries, children under 16 are not normally allowed to work. This tends not to be the case in the developing world where families need the income, and anyway, employment laws are not always so easy to enforce.	Certainly not! Anyway, new businesses are set up all the time, so whenever a computer or robot becomes able to do one kind of work, the world of work adapts. People come up with new ideas and new kinds of work are created.

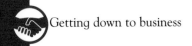
GOOD NEWS...

Enough for everyone!

As developing countries engage in global trade, more people can **afford** all the goods and services people in the developed world already take for granted, like cars, vacations, computers, and other electronic gadgets.

Construction

Buildings require bricks, steel, concrete, wood, glass. They need architects, engineers, and construction workers, too.

Heating

Most of us have heating or air-conditioning in our homes that runs on electricity or gas.

Furniture

Somebody had to make every chair, sofa, bed, table, and dresser in your home.

Water

Water comes out of the faucet thanks to the many workers who maintain the pipes and monitor the water quality.

Clothing

Wool and cotton are grown, harvested, and turned into yarn that is woven into fabric and made into clothes.

Education

The education sector includes teachers, the people who train them, and people who write textbooks.

YOU *the*

Everything you do requires goods or services that other people are involved in providing. The world is full of people producing all you could possibly want or need and getting it to you...

Things that you pay people to do for you *are called SERVICES.*

CONSUMER

Lets take a look at you right now. You may be just sitting quietly reading this book, but have you any idea how many goods and services you are using without even realizing it?

Enough for everyone?
Some scientists believe the Earth cannot **support** us consuming resources at the current rate. They say people in the developed world will have to use less so people in the developing world can enjoy their fair share.

Items that you can buy
are called GOODS.

Energy
Electricity powers most of our appliances. Oil, gas, coal, solar, wind, or nuclear power are used to make electricity.

Farming
If you don't grow your own food, someone else has to. Farmers grow crops and rear animals that we eat.

Telecommunications
Phone and email are very fast-developing technologies. Cell phones were almost unheard of until the 1980s.

Entertainment
TV programs, computer games, books, and music are created by talented people in the entertainment sector.

Transportation
Countless people work in creating, maintaining, and driving (or flying) cars, buses, trains, and planes.

Pharmaceuticals
This industry develops and manufactures drugs that keep many people alive.

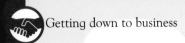

What's what?

There are different kinds of company. But *how* are they *different?* One answer involves seeing who benefits from the profits—family *members*, shareholders, partners, *employees,* customers, a charity, or the general public.

Public company

Members of the public can buy shares making them part-owners in the company. Shareholders make decisions via the directors (who they vote for and who represent them). They receive dividends (a share of the profits) according to how many shares they own.

Partnership

Partners jointly own the company, govern it, share the profits, and are also liable for losses. That means if the company loses money they may have to pay out. Limited partnerships are more common, in which partners aren't personally liable for losses.

Social enterprise

Like a business, a social enterprise aims to make a profit, but its goals go beyond profit. For instance, it may use profit partly to employ certain people (such as those with disabilities) and invest in local social projects.

Franchise

The company has a strong identity and product. It sells licenses to people who want to set up a business and run it themselves using that product. Many fast-food outlets are franchises.

Family business

This is a business owned, controlled, and perhaps even run by members of a family. Family loyalty may be strong, but it can be stressful working with close relatives.

Cooperative

This type of business is owned and controlled by the people who use its services. Each member gets one vote and all issues are decided by a majority vote among the shareholders. They determine how to run the business and how to spend the profits.

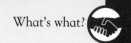

Who are you?

Plenty of businesses are tiny, consisting of just one or two people. Bigger businesses usually *employ* different people to do different jobs, and this creates a whole layer of *management*—people who are in charge of other people. This *"family tree"* shows the management roles in a firm.

I'm the **CEO** (Chief Executive Officer). Sometimes I'm called the **MD** (Managing Director). I'm at the top, and manage the next level down. I am the public face of the company and think ahead about the development of the business.

I'm the **COO** (Chief Operation Officer). I answer to the CEO, and manage the day-to-day running of the company.

I'm the **CFO** (Chief Financial Officer) or Finance Director. My job is keeping track of what the company does with its money.

I'm the Chief **Marketing Officer.** I'm responsible for marketing and advertising our products, public relations, and customer service.

I'm the Chief **Information Officer.** My area is computers, software, and everything to do with sharing and storing information.

I'm the Director of **Human Resources.** I recruit, hire, and evaluate staff. I make sure they get paid and keep track of vacations and benefits.

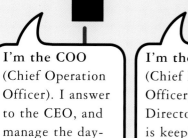

Most companies also have a chairman and a group of people called "the board" made up of various people including executive directors (like the ones described above). Their job is to represent the shareholders of the company by making sure the decisions the CEO makes are legal and in their best interests.

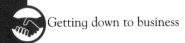

SHAPES and Sizes

Businesses are intriguing things. They are not actually alive, and yet they behave as if they are by growing, adapting, evolving, and sometimes dying. Workers are important to this process, but good leadership is crucial...

STARTING SMALL

Most businesses start with just one person working out of their garage or spare room. Most shut down after a year or two. Setting up a new business involves risk, but good planning makes it more likely to succeed.

> Hi, I'm Reg and I've just set up my own company from home selling tennis balls!

HOW BUSINESSES GROW

Growth normally follows some logical pattern. Here are some of Reg's options for expansion...

- Continue selling tennis balls but try selling more of them.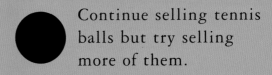

- Sell other types of balls, too.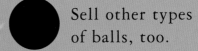

- Sell all kinds of sports equipment.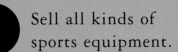

- Hire staff to sell to people at tennis clubs.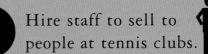

- Get franchisers to sell balls and share profits with you.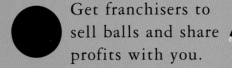

- Buy or merge with another company.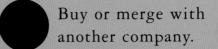

> These days I spend less time actually selling tennis balls and more time thinking about how to make the business grow.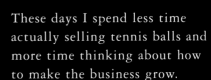

DO THE MATH

In order to succeed, a business has to cover its outgoings—that's the cost of producing the goods or supplying a service—and also generate a profit. It may take time to cover the start-up costs. Eventually, if a business isn't making a good profit, no matter how great its product or service, the business is not sustainable, and will fail.

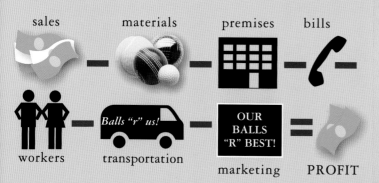

sales — materials — premises — bills

workers — transportation — *Balls "r" us!* — OUR BALLS "R" BEST! marketing = PROFIT

CONGLOMERATES

A conglomerate is a large company made up of lots of different businesses, not all of which have something in common. If you were in the business of buying businesses, why would you become a conglomerate? You'd do this because it means becoming more secure by spreading your risk. Imagine you are buying shares. You wouldn't invest all your money in an umbrella company because if the sun shines you won't do much business. Better to invest some money in an umbrella company and some in a sun-screen business. That way, you're making money whatever the weather.

BUSINESS 2 BUSINESS

Some businesses do much more work with each other than with consumers like you and me. If you sell printers, you can work hard to get a customer to buy one printer, but if you convince a company, they might buy a hundred at once.

x 1   x 100

My strategy now is to get involved in businesses that already exist. I make them run better so they are more profitable.

I work hard but even more importantly, I also work effectively and get results.

Specialization

Expansion isn't for everyone. While some companies are buying or merging with others to form conglomerates, others have chosen to specialize. They spin-off and sell divisions that aren't part of their "core" expertise. That way, they say, they can just focus on doing what they do best.

employs 2.2 MILLION people in 27 countries.

THE *way* we'll WORK

The work we do is utterly unlike the work our grandparents did. Who knows what kind of work our grandchildren will do?

WORK DIARY 2020

JANUARY						
home	office	office	plane	China	China	off
home	office	India	India	home	off	

Where I am working this month and with whom? Let's see...

FULLY WIRED

Technological advances have always driven changes in business. These days communication technologies, like smart phones and Wi-Fi, are changing business so people can work and be contacted at home, on the road, and even in the air. The upside? Terrific flexibility for workers. The downside? Frequent interruptions, and the inability of workers to leave work behind when they are supposed to be sleeping, eating, relaxing, or on vacation.

IT'S A SMALL WORLD

It may be cheaper for a company to set up a factory or a call-center in the developing world and hire workers there than it is for them to pay developed-world costs and wages. Companies operating in more than one country are called multinationals. Some have enormous budgets that make them very powerful. They may be able to influence governments and affect laws regarding working conditions and minimum wages.

Customer service here. How may I help you?

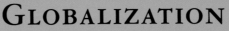

Hello!

GLOBALIZATION

The eventual result of companies operating internationally is that the world becomes one marketplace in which money, labor, and goods flow according to the laws of the free market. To some, globalization is a bad thing because it makes all countries "the same." For others, the benefits are clear since previously poor people sell their goods and skills at a fair price, and rise out of poverty.

Hey everybody! Go with the flow.

CHINA

China is home to 1.4 billion people—a fifth of the world's entire population! It is rich in resources and its economy has been growing rapidly for 25 years. The average income is increasing so fast that each month a million people rise out of poverty. The growth of a massive Chinese middle class will mean a huge new market for consumer goods, cars, and tourism.

We're an economic superpower!

INDIA

India's population—1.25 billion at the moment—is set to overtake China's in around 2050. It is the world's second fastest-growing economy. About 60 percent of people earn their income through farming, but this is also changing. Many educated (and English-speaking) Indians are working in customer service and technical support jobs for overseas firms. Advanced industries such as manufacturing, computer engineering, and biotechnology are flourishing, too.

Soon there'll be more of us than the Chinese.

Must we practice our soft skills on the hard floor?

FLEXIBLE WORKING

The nature of work is changing so fast that there are no more "jobs for life." Instead, people are developing skills that enable them to change jobs frequently or work freelance. Of particular importance are "soft" skills like communication and cooperation. People are working to an older age, not just because life expectancy is longer and they are fit and healthy thanks to medical advances, but also because of the fear that their pensions will be inadequate for their needs.

Surely it's time to stop working. We're both 110!

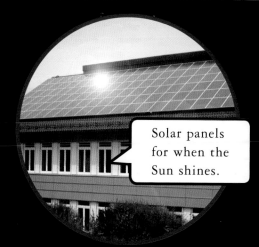

Solar panels for when the Sun shines.

A CHALLENGE WE ALL FACE

The global population is forecast to be 9 billion people by 2050. Will the world be able to support all these people? Growing enough food and generating enough energy for everyone is already a challenge. Concern about climate change and the fragile natural environment are forcing governments to consider just how sustainable continued economic growth is. The search for different energy sources and more sustainable methods of producing and distributing goods are bound to loom large in the future.

From dream...
... to reality

Somebody once said that *invention* is one percent *inspiration* and ninety-nine percent *perspiration*. They weren't joking. To launch a new product you need to be able to convince a lot of people—customers, investors, manufacturers, the press—even if at times you feel less than confident yourself.

Jenny must raise some money

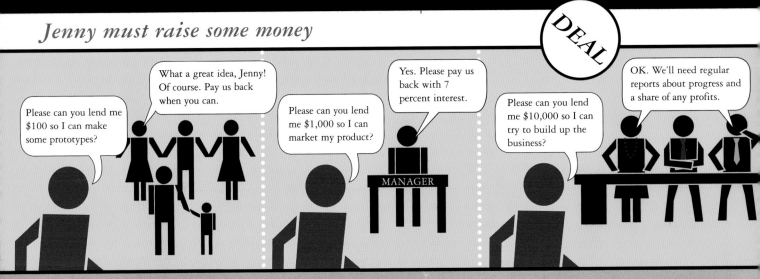

Once upon a time...

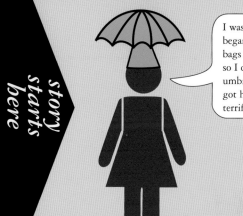

story starts here

I was out and it began to rain. I had bags in both hands so I couldn't hold an umbrella. When I got home I had a terrific idea!

Jenny creates something new.

She makes some calls...

Hello. Is that Umbrellaworld? Would you be interested in stocking a hands-free umbrella?

She researches the market.

One year later

If only it would rain!

The umbrellahats are ready.

Marketing and advertising

Go on posters—spread the word!

That's a good idea!

Raindrops keep falling on your head? You need an Umbrellahat
Call Jenny: 0365 569 8945

Raindrops keep falling on your head? **You need an** **Umbrellahat**
Call Jenny: **0365 569 8945** www.umbrellahat.com

She has to make sure people know about the product...

She thinks about business all the time

New colors? Umbrellahats for pets?!

Could be cool for cats!

Doing more, doing it better...

To be continued...

Running your own business can take over your life. Jenny's constantly figuring out what to do next. She even dreams about umbrellahats. She's got to stay ahead of her competitors, keep existing customers happy, get new customers, and start paying back her investors. She loves the challenge just as much as she loves seeing people wearing her invention.

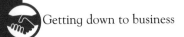

The *LONG* journey to market

Many excellent ideas don't go the distance. To succeed in business you need to be able to play the game.

Research and development

It's often not that simple to make and sell stuff. If you've invented something new, you'll first need to patent your idea so no one else can copy it. Next, you'll need to spend some time on market research—figuring out whether people are likely to buy your product. You'll have to think about how you're going to make and sell it, and once you are making and selling it, you'll need to be thinking ahead about how to improve your product, and what you might make and sell in the future.

Raising capital

It's practically impossible to make money without first spending it. Many new businesses struggle with cashflow—finding enough money to pay the bills before the business is actually selling products and making a profit. What do you do if you have an excellent idea for a business but no money? Figure out what you think you'll need and ask friends and family, the bank, and, finally, professional investors to invest.

"Business is a *game*—the greatest game in the world

Manufacturing

That money you raised? Make sure you've got enough of it to produce a prototype. A prototype is a first attempt at turning the idea into an actual product. Once you've made a prototype you'll be able to see whether the idea actually works and make changes to it if necessary. Eventually (and probably after several prototypes) you should be able to manufacture a small number of units of your product.

Marketing and Advertising

Before you can sell anything you'll need to make sure that potential customers know about your product. How do you reach them? You'll need to do marketing and advertising. Marketing means talking to industries about your product and getting them to direct their customers toward it. Advertising means communicating directly with the people you hope will buy the product by paying for advertisements in the newspapers, magazines, billboards, TV, or radio. You might even have to give some products away so people can try them out and tell you what they think.

Sales

Selling is where the magic really happens. Hopefully you will be able to sell the goods you've made for more than you've spent so far. What's left over is profit. But before you take your share, remember to pay a dividend to your investors, and keep some back to reinvest in the business to cover future costs. To make a real success in the game of business, you need to go on for much longer than just one round...

Business for a better world

Most countries have developed laws to govern businesses and make them fair. People and companies break the law because **unethical business** practices can be **profitable**. Interestingly enough, it seems that good business practices can sometimes turn out to be *even more profitable*. Welcome to the world of **ethical business**.

Putting

people

and the

planet

alongside

profit

THE "TRIPLE BOTTOM LINE"

Some companies now look beyond profit—"the bottom line"—and consider the longer-term sustainability of the way they work. Socially responsible businesses make sure that workers are paid fair WAGES, that WORKING CONDITIONS are appropriate, and don't expose their workers to dangerous chemicals or unsafe equipment. They give workers vacation and sick pay. They don't hire CHILD LABOR. They allow workers to form UNIONS so they can negotiate with management about pay and conditions. They care about their impact on the ENVIRONMENT and make sure their suppliers keep to the same standards they do.

WHAT IS FAIR TRADE?

Many consumers, and even businesses themselves, are ahead of the law in being interested in the ethical side of business. In fact, ethics can even be good for business, since fairer treatment of employees and cleaner production methods often turn out to be profitable, too.

A FAIR price

Developing countries want to sell us their goods, but farm and factory workers can't easily do business with us directly. They rely on middlemen—who skim off a lot of the profit—to arrange deals between them and the big foreign companies who supply us with goods.

For a FAIR product

Fair trade aims to correct this. The Fairtrade organization makes sure that workers and farmers—and not middlemen—get a fair share of the price of their goods. It also sets standards and visits farms and factories to make sure they are kept.

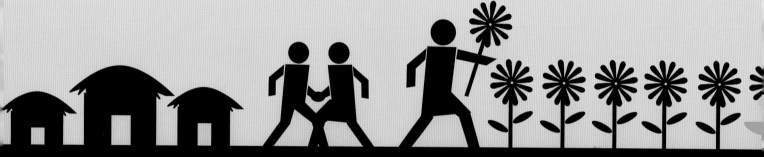

Is fair trade the answer?

Some economists argue that interfering with prices goes against the laws of supply and demand. They prefer to let businesses that can't survive die so workers can turn to producing goods people *are* willing to pay for.

Is free trade the answer?

These economists claim we need *more* free trade, not fair trade. They point out that North American and European subsidies (financial assistance) to local farmers and tariffs (taxes) against foreign ones make it harder for developing countries to sell to us.

Banks for the poor

Muhammad Yunus, a Bangladeshi economist, set up the Grameen Bank to make small loans to very poor borrowers. Low interest rates mean almost all the loans are paid back so the bank profits, and more poor people can be helped.

Consumers are *very powerful* so **think** before you **buy**. SHOPPING with a CONSCIENCE may be one way we can *buy our way to a better world!*

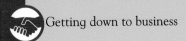

How to SPEND it

People who are very good at making money aren't always so smart when it comes to knowing what to do with it. It's easy to waste money on expensive cars, designer clothes, and fancy restaurants; the trick is finding out how to use money to "buy" greater happiness...

BIG GIVEAWAY

Philanthropy means giving away money, goods, or time to help make the world a better place. Typically, philanthropists have large sums of money to give away. Why do they do it? Well, giving money away can save them on taxes, so that's one reason. But for most, it's also driven by a desire to do something good and help others less fortunate than themselves.

food
money
skills
clothes
time
CHARITY

EXPENSIVE TOYS

Rich people can afford to buy more, bigger, and better houses, cars, vacations, clothes, and jewelry than the rest of us. They can also blow huge amounts on boats and planes if they wish. There's almost no limit to how much money can be spent on a luxurious lifestyle.

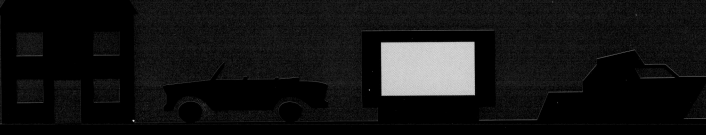

"The man who dies rich dies disgraced."

FUND RESEARCH

The Bill and Melinda Gates Foundation (to which Warren Buffett has also donated generously) has given away $28 billion since its creation in 1994. It assists the world's poorest people in developing countries with vaccines and agricultural improvements. It also helps educationally disadvantaged people in the US.

artists

education

research

development

theater

sports

RAISE AWARENESS

Rock star Bono, of U2, has frequently used his fame to campaign and raise awareness and money. Causes he supports include relieving poverty and disease in Africa, and fighting for human rights in Tibet.

WHO BENEFITS?

There are thousands of deserving causes to support. Philanthropists support religious and educational institutions, scientific research, and help underprivileged and poor people both in their own countries and abroad. Some philanthropists are also patrons of the arts. They help to support artists, writers, musicians, and even sportspeople so they can concentrate on their work instead of worrying about money.

GIVE GRANTS

Oprah Winfrey supports many projects in the US, and has also set up a school in South Africa for gifted girls from poor families.

$5

$10

$20

—*Andrew Carnegie*

87

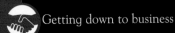 Getting down to business

BILLIONAIRE

One of the best ways to make a fortune is to run your own business. But have you got what it takes? You need to be self-motivated, hardworking, and of course, you have to have a great idea.

STEP 1: HAVE A BRILLIANT IDEA

1 Invent something new.

The paper cup
Lawrence Luellen invented the paper cup in 1908 as a hygienic alternative to the metal cups used at public fountains.

4 Forge good relationships with other businesses.

Microsoft and Intel
Microsoft provides computer operating systems and software, and Intel designs the processors that power computers.

2 Do something better than everyone else.

Pop-up toaster
Toasters existed, but Charles Strite improved them by inventing the pop-up mechanism in 1919 so they no longer needed to be watched.

5 Create a memorable brand.

Google
Google's search engine really works, but having a great name and an instantly recognizable logo has also helped it succeed.

3 Take your product to new customers.

Scooters
Buying a scooter online, 13-year old Dominic McVey decided to buy some extras to sell to friends. Two years later he was a millionaire.

6 Keep control of your brand.

Coca Cola
Tight control of a very well-known brand has kept Coca-Cola the leader in the very competitive cola drinks market.

STEP 2: RUN YOUR BUSINESS BRILLIANTLY

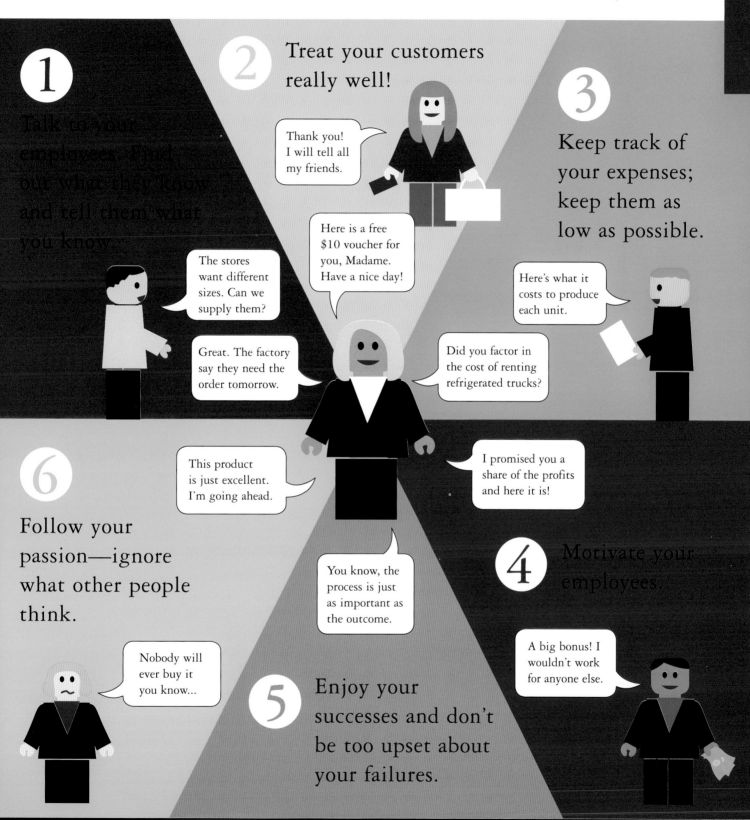

And the WINNERS are...

Here are some of the richest people in the world. They made their fortunes in interesting ways through talent, luck, and sheer hard work.

> *I'm one of the world's richest people.*

BEN AND JERRY
1951–

Ben Cohen and Jerry Greenfield went to school together. At 27, they decided to set up a business making and selling ice cream. Their winning formula involved using local ingredients and sharing the profits with their employees. They sold the company for $326 million in 2000 and now focus on philanthropy.

TIGER WOODS
1975–

Golf player Tiger Woods is the first athlete ever to make $100 million in one year, and became the world's first sports billionaire in 2009. The money came not only from winning tournaments but also from advertising deals. Woods' youth and racial heritage (he is part African-American, Chinese, Dutch, Native American, and Thai) all added to his appeal.

BILL GATES
1955–

Bill Gates experimented with computers from an early age, earning money from programming while still in school. In 1975, he and a friend set up Microsoft, a computer software company. He has been the world's richest man many times, including in 2014 with a fortune of $76 billion. He now works part-time at Microsoft and devotes much of his time to philanthropy.

RICHARD BRANSON
1950–

UK entrepreneur Richard Branson has launched hundreds of companies. He is best known for his airline, Virgin Atlantic, and for various attempts at breaking boating and ballooning world records. In February 2007 Branson announced the Virgin Earth Challenge, which will award $25 million to the person or organization with the best idea for averting global warming.

> I still make a lot of money! I hold the number three slot for dead celebrities after Michael Jackson and Elvis Presley.

> *I bought my own soccer team!*

CHARLES SCHULZ 1922–2000	**J. K. ROWLING** 1965–	**CARLOS SLIM HELU** 1940–	**ROMAN ABRAMOVICH** 1966–
Snoopy, Charlie Brown, and the rest of the Peanuts gang were the creations of cartoonist Charles Schulz. The comic strip ran for nearly 50 years without interruption and appeared in more than 2,600 newspapers in 75 countries. Snoopy made Schulz rich and the cartoon dog continues to make money to this day.	The writer of the Harry Potter books is perhaps the world's most successful living writer. She has sold more than 450 million books and is one of the UK's richest people. The Harry Potter brand is said to be worth $15 billion. The last book in the series came out in 2007 and children throughout the world are waiting to see what she will write next.	This Mexican businessman is the world's second richest man. His fortune was made in the telecommunications business. These days 90 percent of telephone lines in Mexico and 80 percent of cell phones are operated by companies he owns. América Móvil, a cell phone company he owns, has nearly a quarter of a billion subscribers right across Latin America.	Abramovich was born into great poverty in Siberia, Russia. His grandmother brought him up because he was orphaned as a small child. He made his fortune in the Russian oil-mining industry. In addition to doing business, he owns the Chelsea soccer team and owns the world's largest yacht, the *Eclipse*, which cost him $400 million in 2010. He lives mostly in London, England.

Who's *who*?

Economics is quite a young science. It only got a name (and that name was actually *Political Economy*) in the 18th century when the financial side of how countries behaved started to interest philosophers.

> *A debt should be paid off till the last penny.*

> From each according to his abilities, to each according to his needs.

CHANAKYA 350–283 BCE	**ADAM SMITH** 1723–1790	**THOMAS MALTHUS** 1766–1834	**KARL MARX** 1818–1883
Perhaps the world's first economist was Chanakya. This wise philosopher and smart politician was responsible for creating the first Indian empire. Some consider his *Arthashastra* (The Science of Material Gain) the world's first economics textbook. In it, he discusses his thoughts on welfare, international relations, and war strategies.	Smith believed that self-interest was a good thing in a free market where the goods that people wanted would be made and sold at the appropriate price. That's not to say he saw no role for governments. In fact, he believed that governments were necessary to prevent collusion (businesses ganging up together to cheat customers) and to provide public goods.	Malthus wrote "An Essay on the Principle of Population." In it he described how the world's population would grow hugely, resulting in starvation and poverty. He was very influential. Though he was right in predicting massive growth (and explaining the math behind it), he did not realize that technological improvements would enable us to keep from starving.	Marx believed that the free-market economy (which he called capitalism) took advantage of the majority of people who were workers and not business- or land-owners. He predicted that in the end the workers would revolt. His political philosophy inspired revolutions and created communism, a political system that is still used in China and North Korea.

EVERY SHORT STATEMENT ON A BROAD ISSUE IS INHERENTLY FALSE.

The importance of money flows from it being a link between the present and the future.

I am in favor of cutting taxes under any circumstances and for any excuse, for any reason, whenever it's possible.

ALFRED MARSHALL 1842–1924

JOHN MAYNARD KEYNES 1883–1946

MILTON FRIEDMAN 1912–2006

JOHN FORBES NASH 1928–2015

The originator of the idea of supply and demand brought real mathematical proof to the ideas expressed by Adam Smith. Although he was an accomplished mathematician, he insisted that economists express their ideas with real-life examples. This way, people with no specialized knowledge of math could understand them.

This English economist's big idea was that governments should intervene in financial crises by spending money to stimulate the economy and set a recovery in motion. He was very influential, and this policy was adopted during the long years of the US's Great Depression in the 1930s, and is still very popular in the UK today.

This American Nobel laureate disagreed with Keynes and felt that the freedom of the free market should never be undermined by government intervention. He claimed that economic freedom, when introduced into a society, would in the end give rise to political freedom. His *laissez faire* policies were widely and successfully practiced.

An American mathematician, Nash invented game theory, and was joint winner of a Nobel Prize. Game theory is useful for understanding situations where people make choices based on what they know or *think* they know about the choices other people are making. A game of cards works like this, and so does an auction—bidders base their own bids on what they expect other bidders will do.

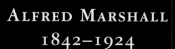

"Freedom to Choose"

GLOSSARY

advertising way to let potential customers know about a product or service and encourage them to buy it.

ATM (Automated Teller Machine) machine that allows customers to check their accounts and take out money

barter a way of trading goods that does not involve money.

bill piece of paper requesting payment.

bank institution that looks after customers' money and lends money to people and businesses.

banknote paper money.

black market illegal buying and selling of goods.

bond financial product that allows an investor to loan money to a business or organization in exchange for regular interest payments.

brand name or logo that is associated with a particular company's goods or services.

bureau de change place to buy or sell foreign currencies.

capitalism economic system driven by the free market and peoples' desire to make money.

command economy economic system where supply and price are regulated by the government.

communism social and economic system based on shared ownership of resources.

compound interest interest earned on a sum of money and on the interest it has already generated.

conglomerate large company owning many smaller (and often unrelated) companies.

consumer person who buys a good or a service.

cost money used up in making something.

credit card card that allows consumers to buy goods using borrowed money, and pay for them later.

currency anything that is widely accepted as money.

debit card card that immediately deducts money from the card-holder's account when they make a purchase.

debt money (or something else) that one person or organization owes to another.

demand amount of products or services consumers would like to buy.

discount amount by which an item is selling below its normal price.

economics social science studying the production, distribution, and consumption of goods and services.

economist expert in the field of economics.

employer person or organization that hires workers.

entrepreneur someone who has ideas for and creates new businesses.

equilibrium price price at which supply and demand are matched so most goods are sold at the best price.

euro unit of currency used throughout much of Europe.

expansion increase in the level of economic activity, and of goods and services available, in the market place.

fair trade way of doing business intended to ensure that producers receive a fair price for their goods.

franchise business in which people buy licenses to trade using someone else's brand.

free market economic system with few regulations, running according to the laws of supply and demand.

fiat money coins or paper currency that are worth more than the value of the materials they are made from.

future financial product for buying or selling a good in the future at a price agreed upon now.

globalization process in which the whole world moves toward doing business (and other things) in the same way.

gold standard financial system where the value is money is related to the value of gold.

goods items that producers make and consumers buy.

GDP (Gross Domestic Product) amount of goods a country produces.

human resources people who work to make a product or provide a service.

incentive reason for choosing one thing over another.

inflation rise in the price of goods and services that is higher than the rise in peoples' wages.

insurance financial product that pays out in the event of loss or accident.

interest amount of money paid by people who borrow money to the people who lend it to them.

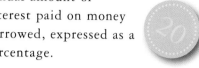

interest rate annual amount of interest paid on money borrowed, expressed as a percentage.

investment placing money in a business or financial product with the hope of making more money.

laissez faire economic policy of interfering with the free market as little as possible.

manufacture making things to use or to sell.

marketplace the space where a market operates. It does not need to be an actual location.

marketing process of finding out what consumers want and trying to influence demand.

merchant person whose role is buying and selling rather than producing.

middleman a term for the businessman or woman who organizes a deal between a producer and seller and takes a share of the profits.

mint place where coins are made.

mortgage financial product that allows a person to buy a house and pay for it over a number of years.

multinational company that works in more than one country.

natural resources products from the earth, sea, or air used to create goods.

pension financial product that pays out money to people who have retired from work.

philanthropy the act of contributing money or time to make the world a better place.

price amount of money a seller asks for a unit of goods.

producer person who makes a good or supplies a service.

profit difference between the cost of bringing a product to market and the price at which it is sold.

prosperity wealth itself, or a period of time in which the economic wealth of a country is growing.

recession period of at least six months when the economy of a country is shrinking.

recovery period in which a country's economic growth is emerging from a recession.

resources raw materials used to create a good or service.

retirement point when a person stops earning money from full-time work.

saving accumulating money in a bank or savings and loan where it is not at risk of loss.

services some things sold to consumers by producers or suppliers; these aren't goods that can be seen or touched.

share way of owning a small part of a company and sharing in any profits.

shareholder person who owns a share in a company.

stock same as a share.

stock exchange place where shares are bought and sold.

sunk cost money and time spent on creating a good or service that cannot be recovered.

supply amount of goods or services available to consumers.

subsidy form of financial assistance paid, often by the government, to keep prices below what they would be in a free market.

tariff tax charged for bringing goods in to sell in a foreign country.

tax money demanded by the government.

trade buying and selling of goods.

union group of workers who have banded together to achieve better pay or working conditions.

value what people believe a good or service is worth.

wage what a person is paid for their work.

INDEX

I'll take 20 crates of your oranges.

Acknowledgments

Dorling Kindersley would like to thank the following people for help with this book: Chris Bernstein, Sean Daly, Sasha Frieze, Elinor Greenwood, Lorrie Mack, Myriam Megharbi, Gabriel Rozenberg, Penny Smith, Ben Taxman

The publisher would like to thank the following for their kind permission to reproduce their photographs:

(Key: a-above; b-below/bottom; c-centre; f-far; l-left; r-right; t-top)

Alamy Images: Ace Stock Limited 78bl; blickwinkel 79bl; culliganphoto 90br; Ann Cutting 8bl; Dacology 88crb; Chad Ehlers 25clb, 78tl; Kevin Foy 90bl; David Hancock 88br; Horizon 66-67t; Imagebroker/Stefan Obermeier 88cr; Huw Jones 25tl; K-PHOTOS 18crb; Dan Lamont 90cra; Mary Evans Picture Library 15cr, 91tc, 92cr; Barry Mason 1bc, 9cl, 30tr, 34br, 47bc; James Osmond 48crb, 62-63c; Panorama Media (Beijing) Ltd 12cr; Chris Pearsall 43cl (shoe); David Pearson 78cl; Photos 12 91bl; Phototake Inc. 70fcr, 84cl (Doctor); The Print Collector 13tc; PSL Images 25tr, 92bl; Andrew Rubtsov 9bc; Marco Secchi 91cla; Glyn Thomas 21fcra (Five Singapore dollars), 21fcra (Two Singapore dollars); Visions of America, LLC 21cra (Ten US dollars); Visual Arts Library (London) 16cl; Visual Arts Library (London) / Indian school, (3rd century BC) 92fbl; WoodyStock 32l; David Young-Wolff 79clb; **Ancient Art & Architecture Collection:** Ronald Sheridan 12bl; **ATM Industry Association:** 19br; **Bank of Canada:** 21crb (Canadian dollars); **The Bridgeman Art Library:** Private Collection 15bc; **Corbis:** Bettmann 15crb, 16bl, 18cra, 56bl, 92cl, 93cl; Keith Dannemiller 91cra; Araldo de Luca 12br; Yves Forestier 19tr; Andrew Gompert/epa 91fcra; Hulton-Deutsch Collection 17fcr, 92fcr; Wolfgang Kaehler 20cr; Justin Lane/epa 90fcra; Christian Liewig 85bl; Paul Mounce 90cla; Richard T. Nowitz 90fcla; Charles O'Rear 18clb, 20b, 21b, 22bl;

Perrin Pierre/Corbis Sygma 17bl; Roger Ressmeyer 93cr; Reuters 91fcla; Joseph Sohm/Visions of America 21cra (Twenty US dollars); Paul Souders 79tl; Stephen Welstead 30c; Haruyoshi Yamaguchi 71fcr; Naashon Zalk 87tr; Peter Adams/zefa 79cla; **De La Rue:** 22c, 22clb, 22crb, 22cr-23cl, 23cb, 23cla; **Diners Club International Ltd/Citibank International plc:** 19cl, 30tl (Diners Club Card), 33cb, 33fcra (Diners Club Card); **www.dinodia.com:** 92fcl; **DK Images:** Bank of Ulster 22bc, 23bl; British Museum 12c, 13c, 13cl, 13cr, 20cl, 23cr, 23fcra; The British Museum 51br (Silver coin); The British Museum 51bc (Gold coin), 51cra; Chas Howson/The British Museum 17cr; Museum of Mankind/British Museum 20c; Royal Australian Mint 20ftr, 21tc (Australian coin); James Stevenson/Courtesy of the National Maritime Museum, London 15tr; Michel Zabe 15br; **Dreamstime.com:** Dreamstimegreat 43bcr (smart phone), Empire331 43bc (camera), Kósa Tibor 25cl (phone); **Getty Images:** Sven Creutzmann/Mambo Photography 92fbr; Steve Granitz/WireImage 87crb; VisionsofAmerica/Joe Sohm 26-27cb; John Macdougall 67cl; K Mazur/WireImage 87ca; Ryan McVay/Stone 70cl, 84fcl (Workman); Peter Ruck/Hulton Archive 19bl; Photographer's Choice/Sean Ellis 72bc; Photonica/Flynn Larsen 88bl; Steven Puetzer 26cl; Roy Stevens//Time Life Pictures 19tl; Bob Strong/AFP 93fcr; Hiroshi Watanabe 27tr; **The Marshall Library of Economics, University of Cambridge:** 93fcl; **Photolibrary:** Neil Duncan 14cl; **Planetary Visions:** 79tr, 78bl (globe); **PunchStock:** Photodisc 71cl; Photodisc/Dan Tero 68c; **The Royal Mint, Crown Copyright:** 22cla, 22tl

All other images © Dorling Kindersley

For further information see: www.dkimages.com